CRICUT MAKER IDEAS!

SIMPLE IDEAS FOR MAKING FANTASTIC PROJECTS WITH YOUR CRICUT MAKER

Made with love

by

Sienna

Tally

TABLE OF CONTENTS

Introduction

Dear Readers,

Thank you for purchasing this handy guide to begin a creative journey with me and your Cricut Maker. Inside "Cricut Maker: Ideas!" you'll find plenty of ideas to get you started on your projects with ease and harmony.

In the year 2017, a new model in the Cricut family was released called The Cricut Maker™. This has all the bells and whistles to do most anything. It can cut more materials than any previous models, and the company boasts its fast, precise cutting.

The Cricut Maker is considered to be Cricut's flagship model. This is the one that can do just about anything under the sun on just about any material you can fit into the mat guides of your machine. The one drawback of this powerhouse model is the price point. This does make this model more prohibitive unless you plan to create crafts that you can sell with this model. If this is your intention, you can rest assured that whatever you turn out with this machine will be the best of the best, every single time. If you're selling your crafts, this baby will pay for itself in little to no time at all.

With that in mind, the Cricut Maker costs $399.99. That is a large sum of money for someone who doesn't have it and even someone who does have it. Although there's a lot you can do with $399.99, there are just as many things you can do with the Cricut Maker. My advice would be to save until you can afford it or put it on your wishlist in the meantime and subtly hint to your loved ones that you'll love to have one of these bad boys. Hopefully, someone will catch on and not balk at the massive amount of dollars that it will eat up.

The Cricut Maker can be used with your images, a plus for those who prefer to use their own or don't want to buy a subscription or pay for individual photos. It allows you to personalize your items and make your statement. You can create personalized cards, signs, and anything your heart desires. The ability to personalize your items with multiple lines and fonts broadens your horizon, and if you make products to sell, you can offer personalization.

From Sienna Tally, happy reading!

BASIC TOOL KIT

All the five essential tools in one package:
- A scraper to clean and polish
- Spatula to lift
- Micro-tip scissors
- Weeder for vinyl
- Tweezers

BASICS STARTER TOOL KIT

Another set of essential tools including:
- Scraper and spatula
- Point pens in metallic
- Scoring stylus
- Deep Cut Housing and one blade

ESSENTIAL TOOL KIT

Made for Cricut Explore models, this 7-piece set includes:
- Trimmer and replacement blade
- Scoring stylus

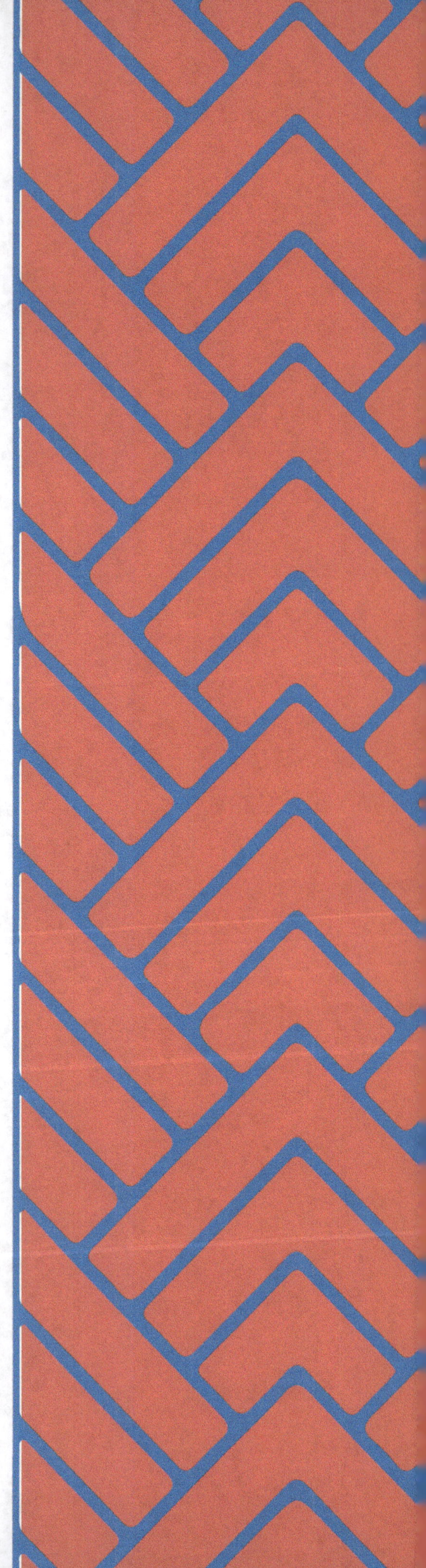

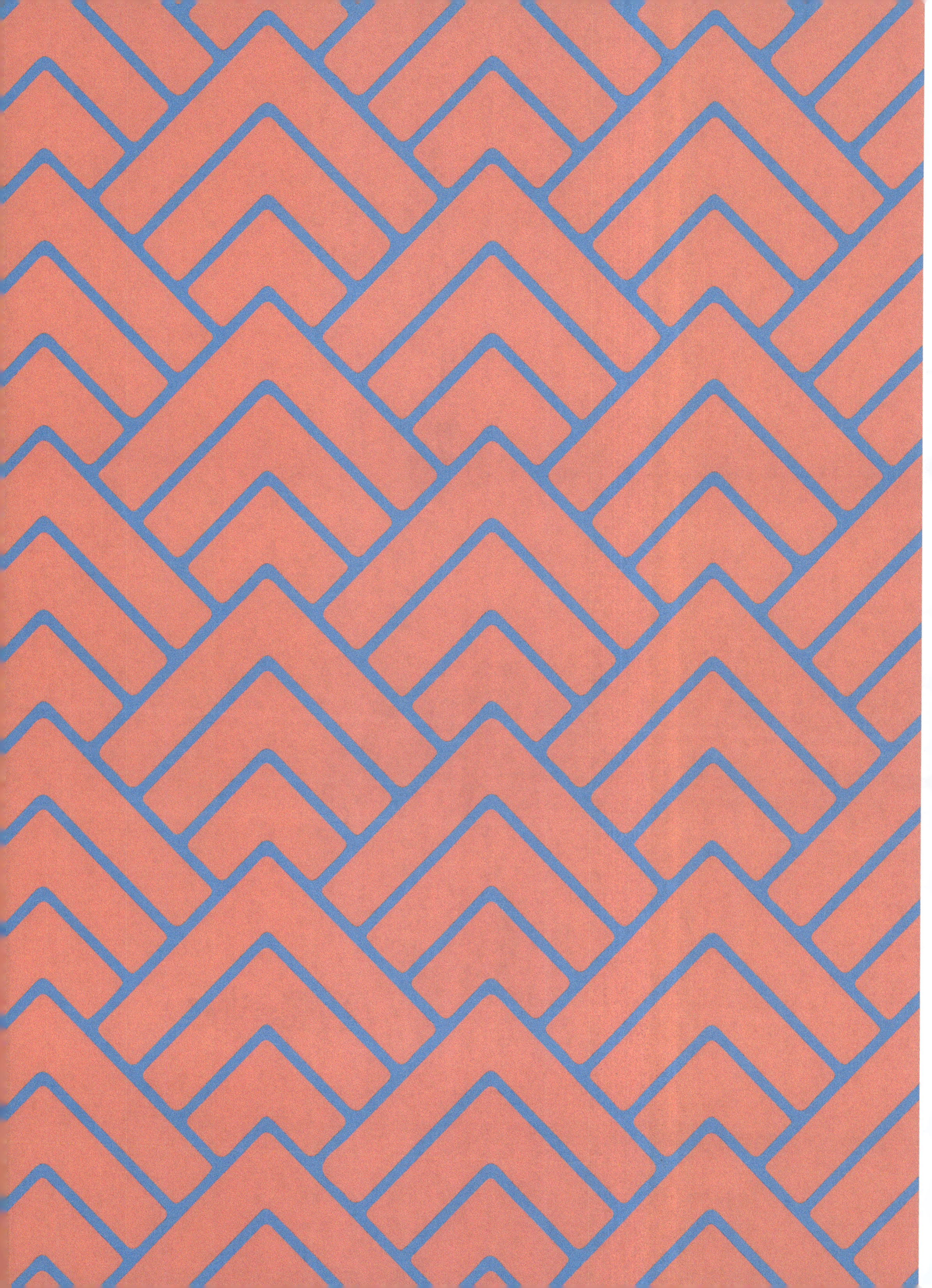

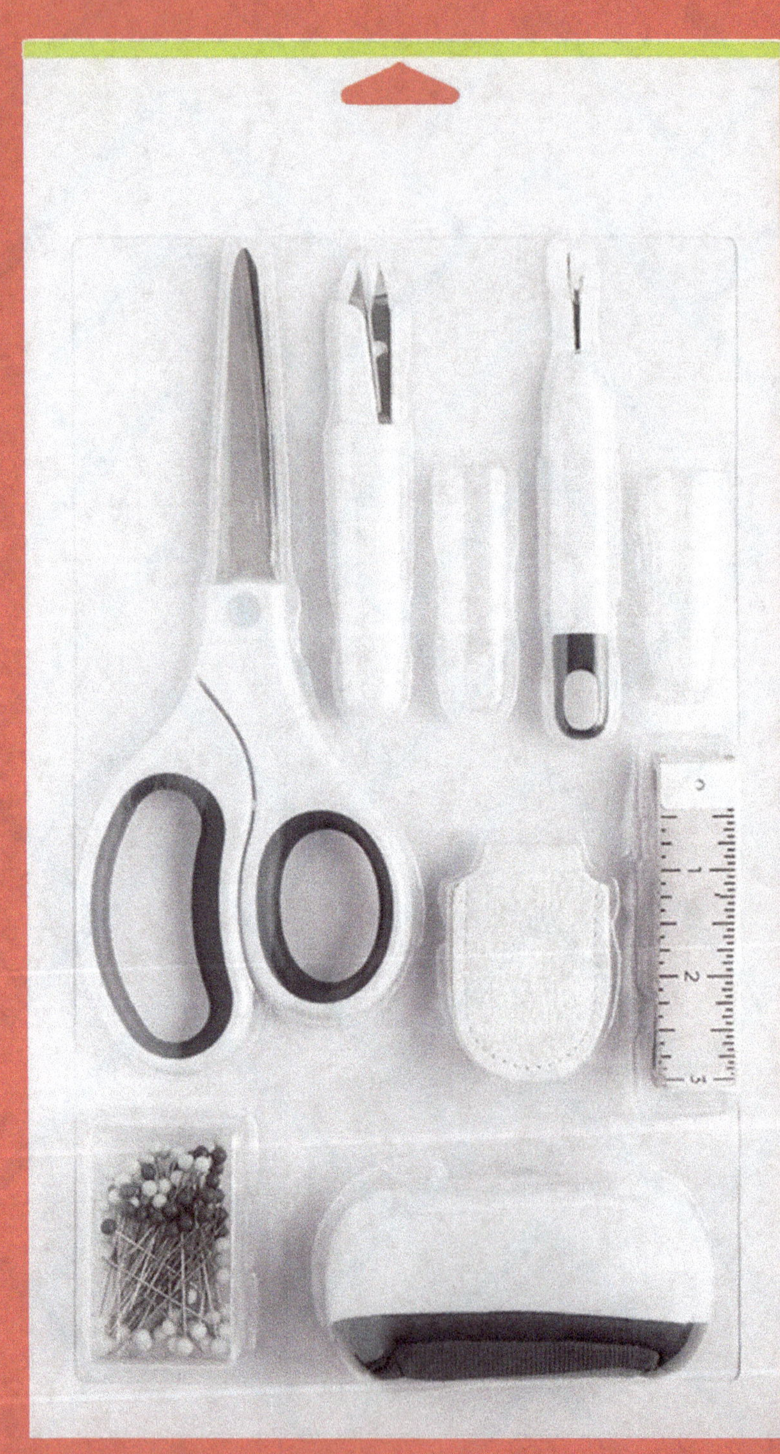

- Scraper for cleaning and polishing
- Spatula
- Micro-blade scissors
- Weeder
- Tweezers

PAPER CRAFTING TOOL KIT

This 4-piece set is perfect for professional paper crafting and includes:
- Craft mat
- Distresser for edges
- Quilling tool for spirals
- Piercer for small piece placement

SEWING TOOL KIT

Sewing essentials are all in one place. This set includes:
- Thimble made of leather
- Measuring tape
- Pins and pincushion
- Seam ripper
- Thread snips
- Fabric shears

WEEDING TOOL KIT

A set of 5 tools for elaborate cutting and vinyl DIY crafts includes;
- Hook tweezers
- Fine tweezers
- Hook weeder

- Weeder
- Piercer

COMPLETE STARTER TOOL KIT

Perfect for the beginning Cricut user, this set includes:
- Black window cling
- Cutting mat
- Point pens in metallic
- Scoring stylus
- Deep Cut Housing and 1 Blade
- A scraper to clean and polish
- Spatula to lift
- Micro-tip scissors
- Weeder to remove negatives
- Tweezers

SINGLE TOOLS

XL SCRAPER

Clean mats quickly and easily or adhere sizeable projects to an assortment of surfaces with this tool. Great for vinyl and can be used with all Circuit models.

PORTABLE TRIMMER

Precision cutting is achieved with the 12-inch swinging arm, and the storage for a replacement blade makes this an extra-functional tool. Swiftly insert materials, cut, and measure from both directions with

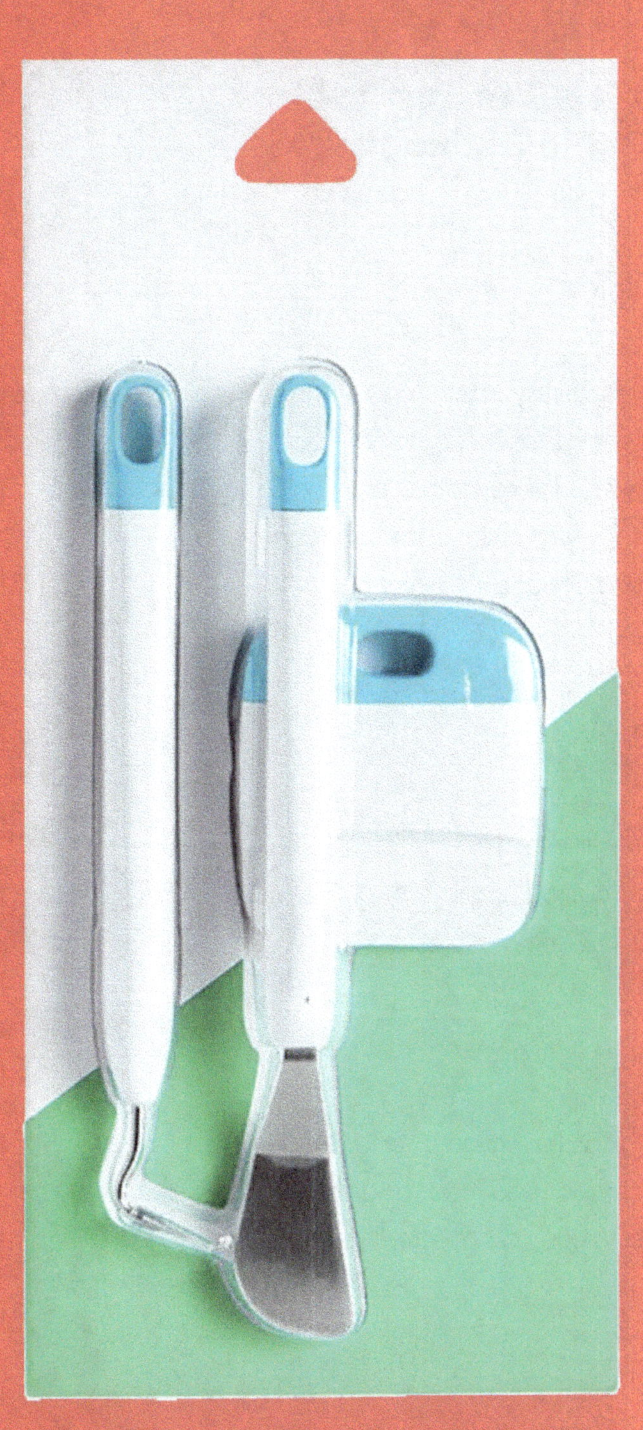

the dual-hinged rails.

SCORING STYLUS

3-dimensional projects, boxes, cards, and envelopes' lines can be scored in 1 step with this tool
that holds the blade for cutting and the stylus.

APPLICATOR AND REMOVER

Remove or apply textiles easily and make the
cutting mat last longer with these functional tools.
Ideal for the Cricut Maker, these tools are sold
together to make working with fabric that much
more comfortable (applicator is also known as a
brayer).

SCRAPER AND SPATULA

Lift and clean easily with these two tools. It was
made especially for the cutting mat for all sorts
of projects.

SCISSORS

Make clean cuts with micro-tip scissors and store
them safely with the included end cap and cover
for the blades (you can use a medical scissor
too).

TWEEZERS

Secure project pieces after lifting them with the
reverse-grip of this tool. Perfect to use for small

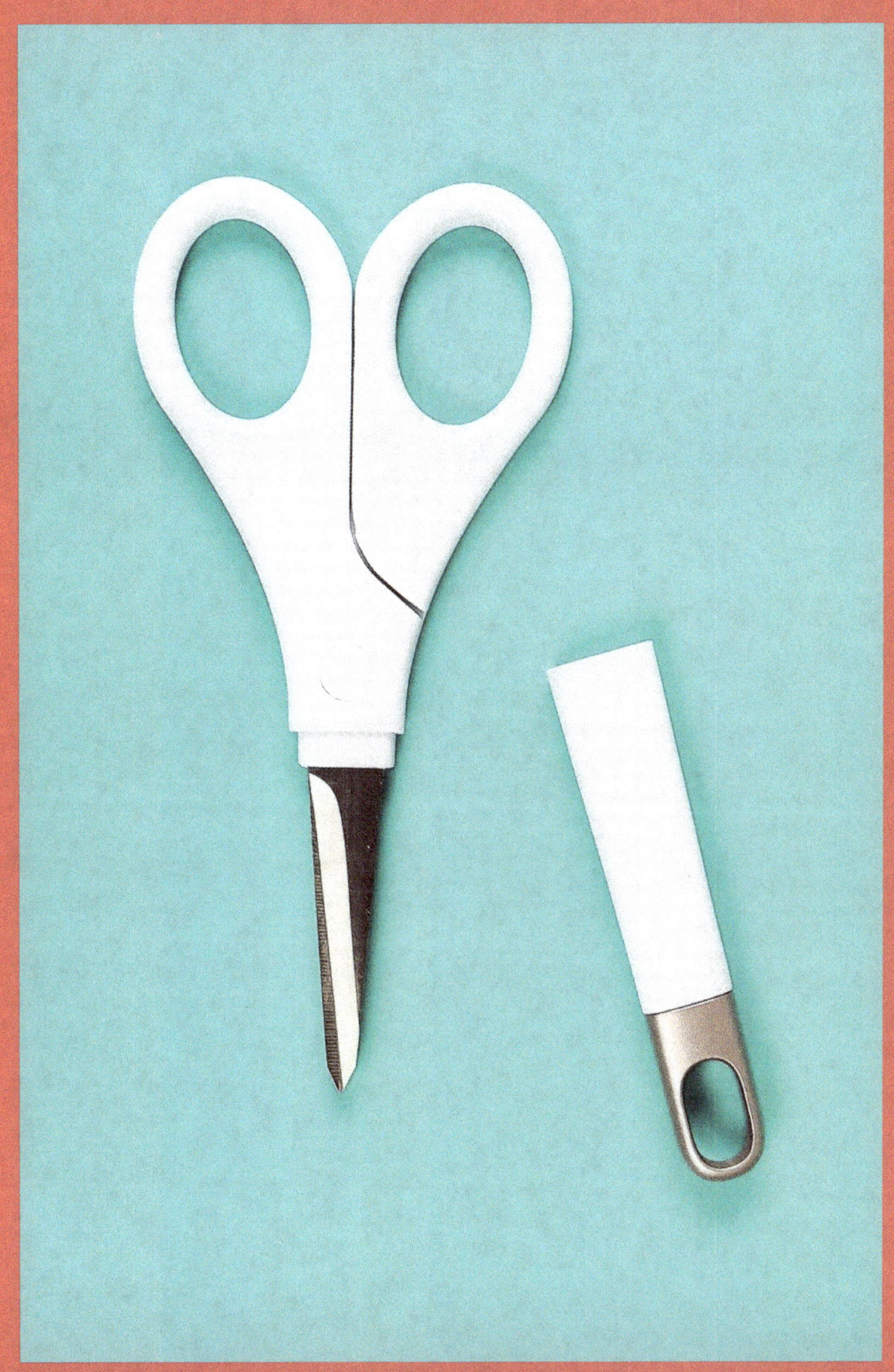

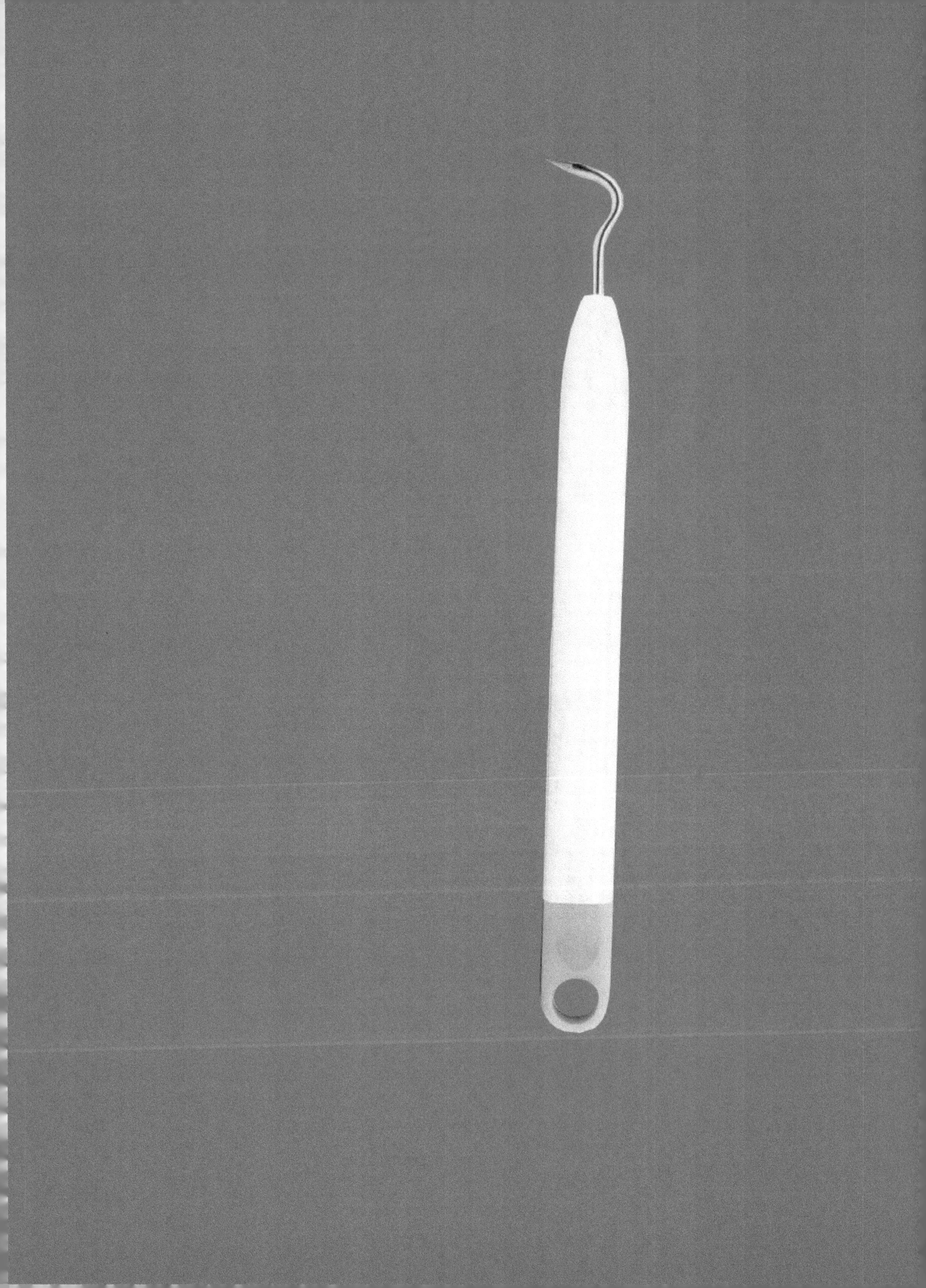

items like small cuts and intricate trimmings.

WEEDERS

Use this tool to remove small cuts and sepa-
rate iron-on pieces and vinyl from their liners.

ACCESSORIES

Below is a list that highlights some of the
available accessories and their functions. Consider purchasing them individually or take
advantage of the different bundles and sets
offered.

FUNCTIONAL SUPPORT ACCESSORIES

Specially designed accessories are made to
enhance the experience of using a Cricut
machine with function and style.

- Mats
- Light grip
- Standard grip
- Strong grip
- Fabric grip
- Scoring and Blades
- Rotary blade
- Fabric blade-bonded
- Deep cut blade
- Fine-point blade
- Premium blade made of German
  carbide
- Scoring stylus

PENS

- Variety of colored pens
- Extra fine tip-colored pens
- Ultimate fine tip-colored pens
- Washable fabric pen
- Variety of colored markers

TAPES

- Glitter tape
- Adapters and Tech
- Cartridge adapter
- Pen adapter
- Bluetooth adapter
- Accessory adapter
- USB cable
- Power cord
- Keyboard overlay

These accessories are the perfect fit for the crafter on the go or in need of stylish and functional storage.

POUCHES

- Accessory pouches for tools
- Totes and Bags
- Crafters shoulder bag
- Rolling crafters tote
- Machine tote
- Machine Add-On's

Cricut machines can accomplish many great thin-

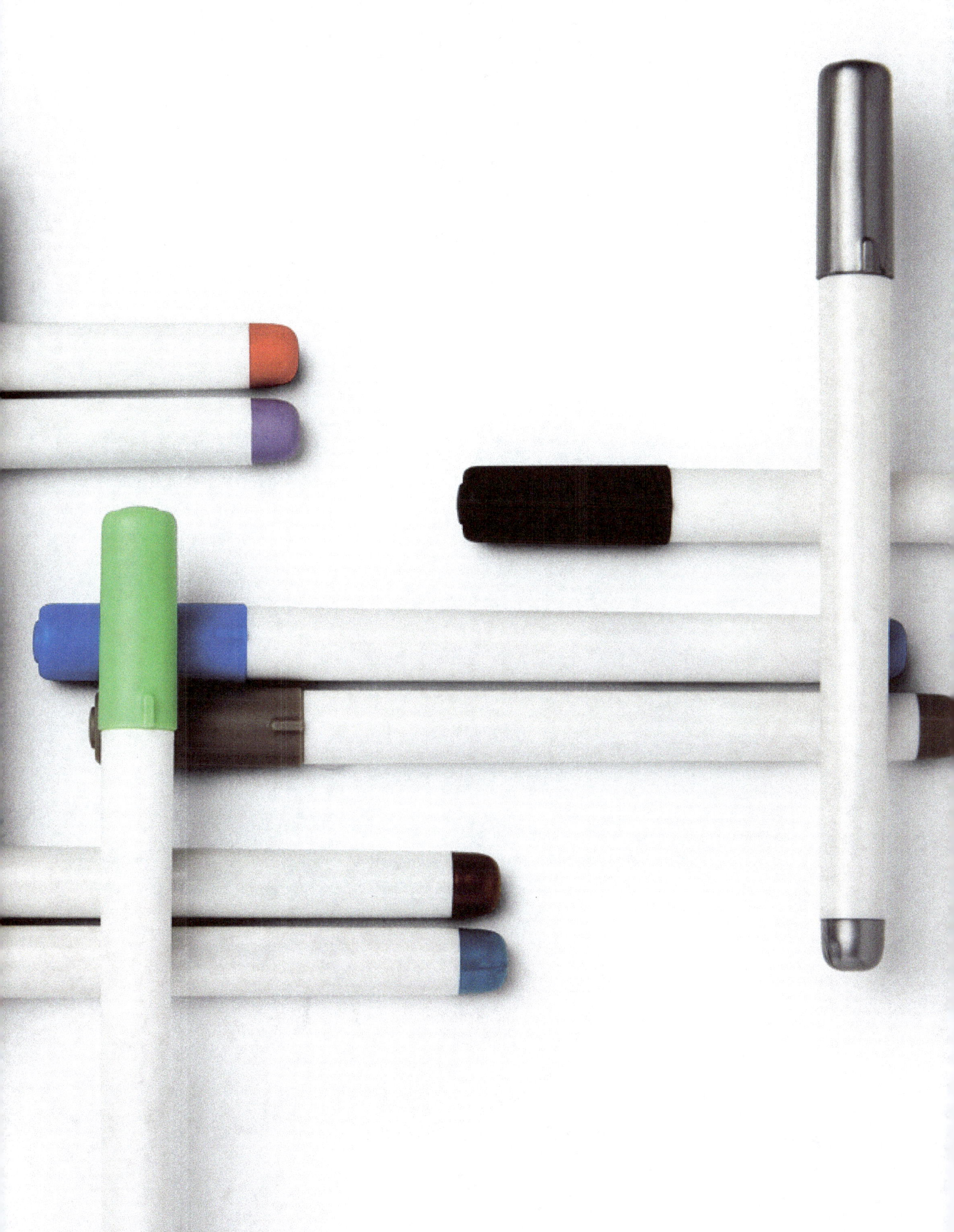

gs, but sometimes they could use a sidekick. That's where these machines come in.

EASY PRESS

Achieve the iron-on results like a professional in less than a minute! Simple to use and light to carry, this accessory is perfect for Cricut users who want t-shirt transfers to last.

EASY PRESS BUNDLES:

- Bulk
- Ultimate
- Everything

CUTTLEBUG

Cut or emboss almost any material on the run with this handy machine. Achieve the professional, clean cuts you want with ease.
Cuttlebug Add-ons:

- Mats
- Dies
- Materials
- Spacer plates
- Cutting mats

BRIGHT PAD

This durable, light pad offers a soft, adjustable light to make tracing cutting and more manageable and more comfortable on the eyes.

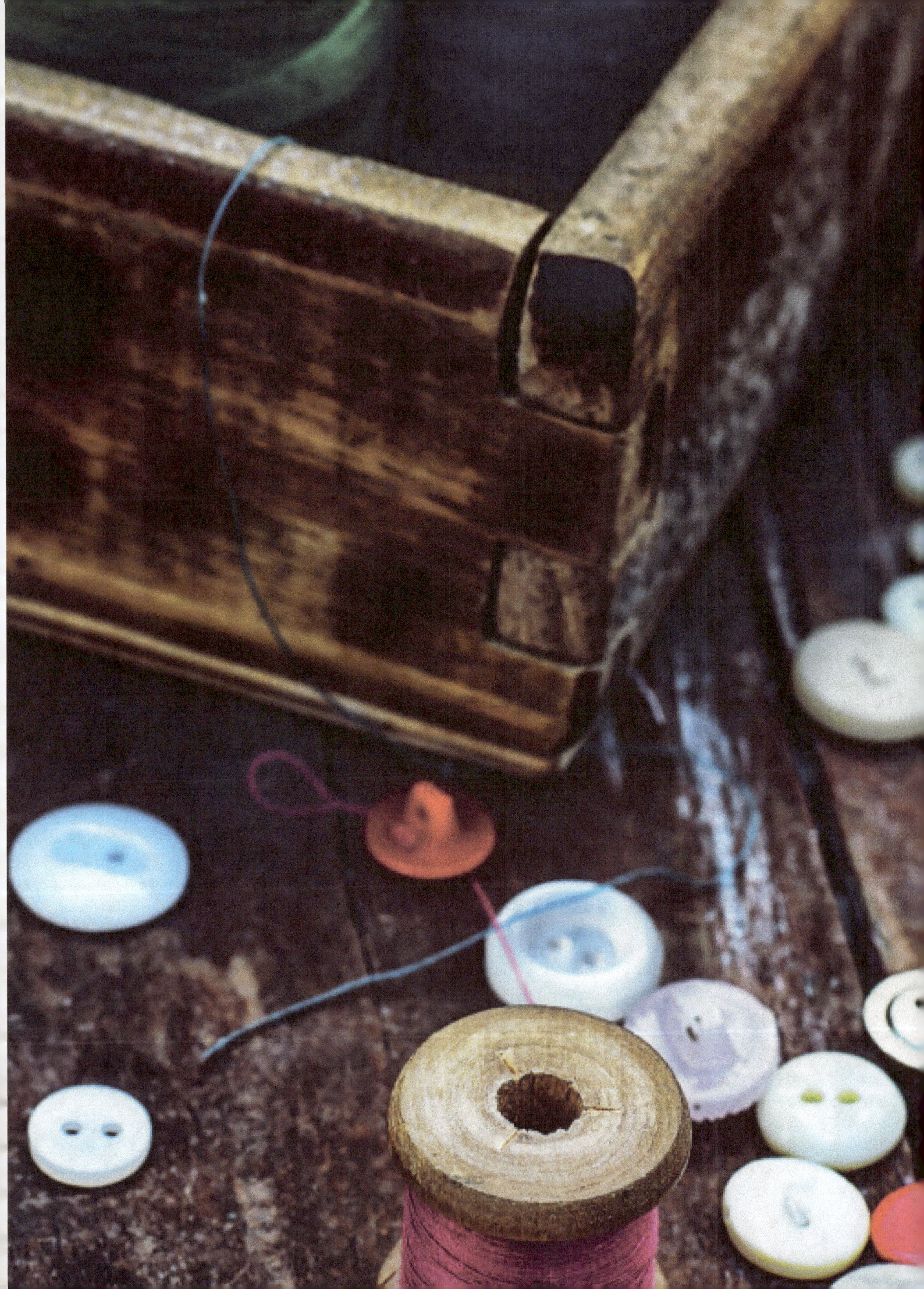

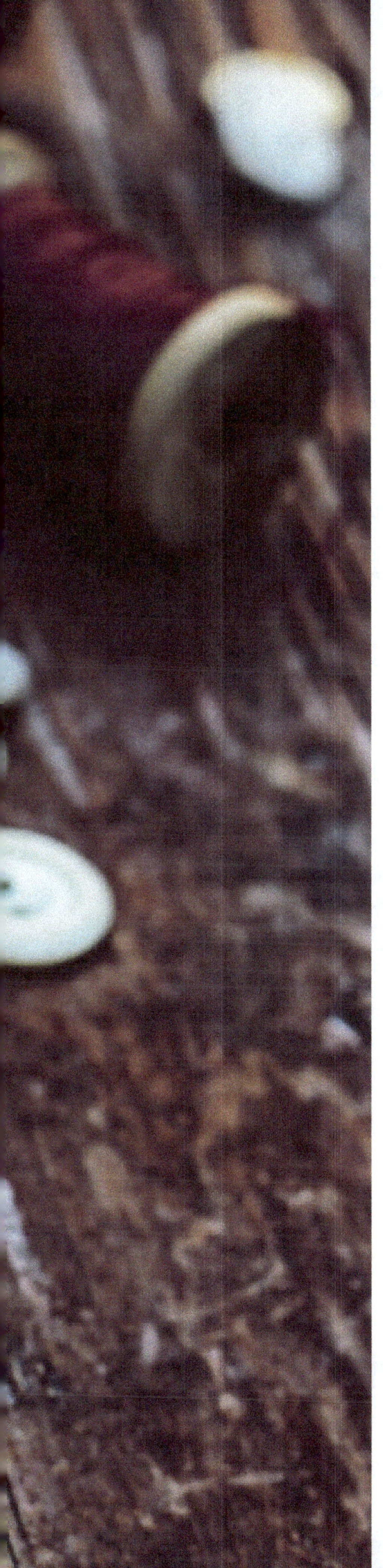

Chapter 2
Cricut Maker Tools Mainte nance and Care

After a while, you may notice some of your projects coming out in a condition that is less-than-crisp. In this section, I'll outline a troubleshooting and maintenance checklist you can utilize to bring your Cricut machine back into peak working condition!

1. ENSURE YOUR MACHINE IS ON A STABLE FOOTING.

This may seem pretty basic, but ensuring that your machine is on a level surface will allow it to make more precise cuts every single time. The rocking of the device or wobbling could cause inconsistent results in your projects.
Ensure no debris has gotten stuck under the feet of your machine that could cause instability before proceeding to the next troubleshooting step!

2. REDO ALL CABLE CONNECTIONS

So, your connections are in the best possible working order, undo all your cable connections, blow into the ports or use canned air, and then securely plug everything back into the right ports. This will help to make sure all the connections are talking to each other where they should be!

3. COMPLETELY DUST AND CLEAN YOUR MACHINE

Your little Cricut works hard for you! Return the favor by making sure you're not allowing gunk, dust, grime, or debris to build up in the surfaces and crevices. Adhesive can build up on the machine around the mat input and on the rollers, so be sure to focus on those areas!

If you have a can of compressed air, use it to blast any small parts and pieces of material or dust that may have built up around the cutting strip, bar and rollers, and mat input. Q-Tips can also be an excellent resource for cleaning out the small spaces in your machine; put that rubbing alcohol to use further!

4. CHECK YOUR BLADE HOUSING

Sometimes debris and residue from your materials can build up inside the housings for your blades! Open them up and clear any built-up materials that could be impeding swiveling or motion.

5. SHARPEN YOUR BLADES

A trendy Cricut trick in use is to stick a clean, fresh piece of foil to your Cricut mat and run it through with the blade you wish to sharpen. Running the blades through the thin metal helps revitalize their edges and give them a little extra staying power until it's time to buy replacements.

Another way to do this is to make a foil ball, remove the blades from the housing, and stick them into the foil ball several times until you notice a

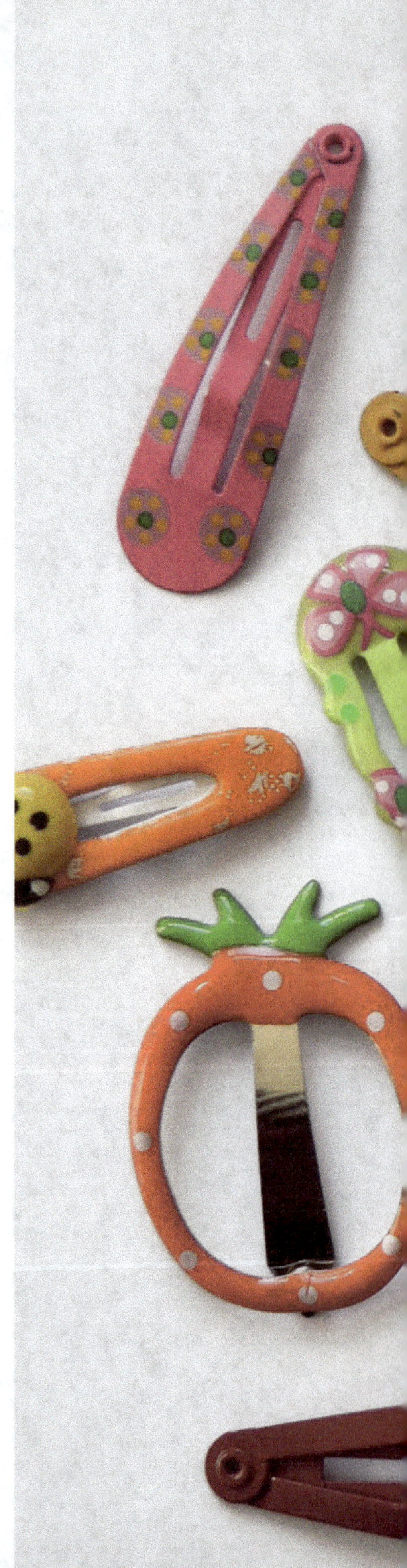

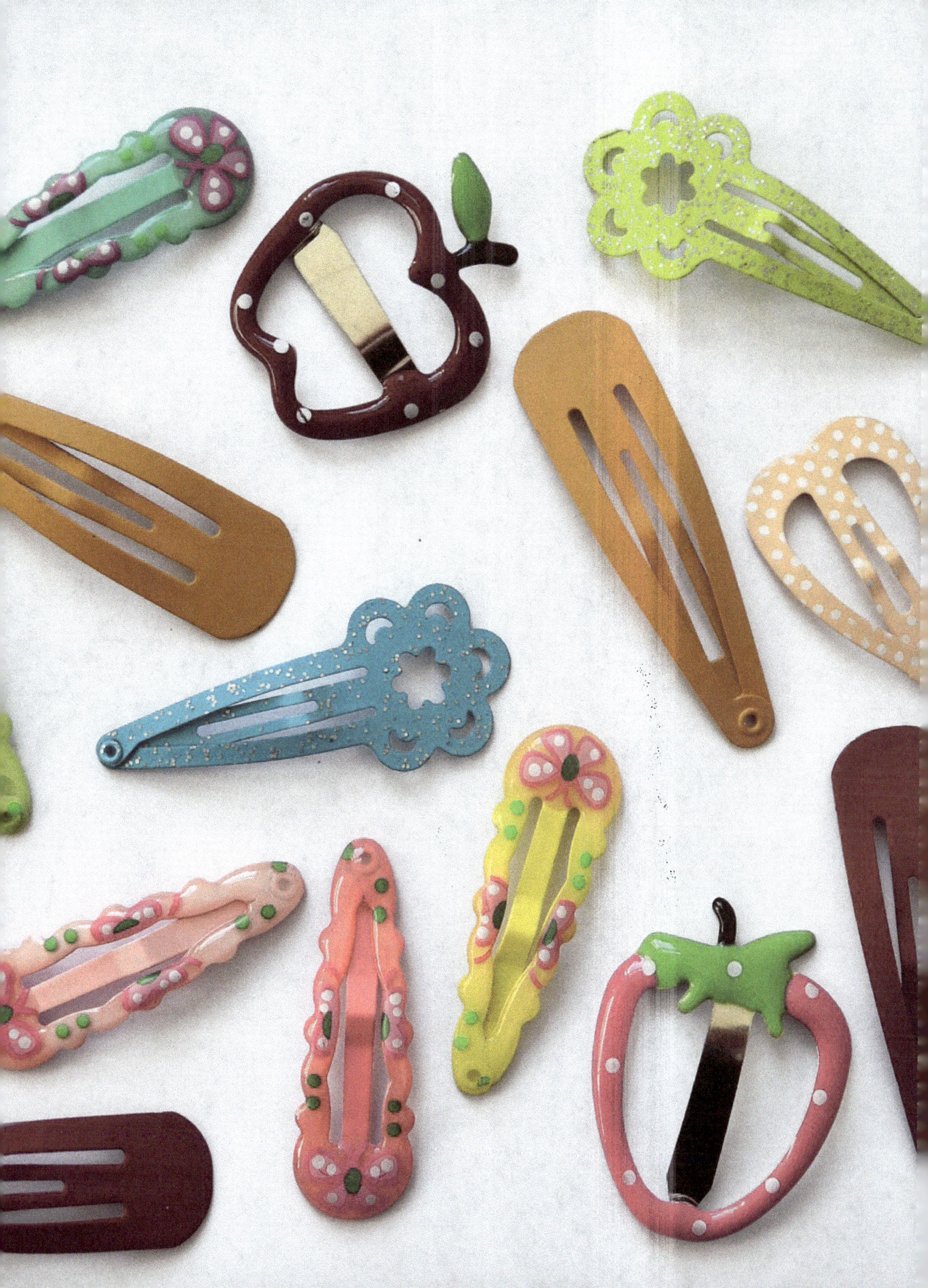

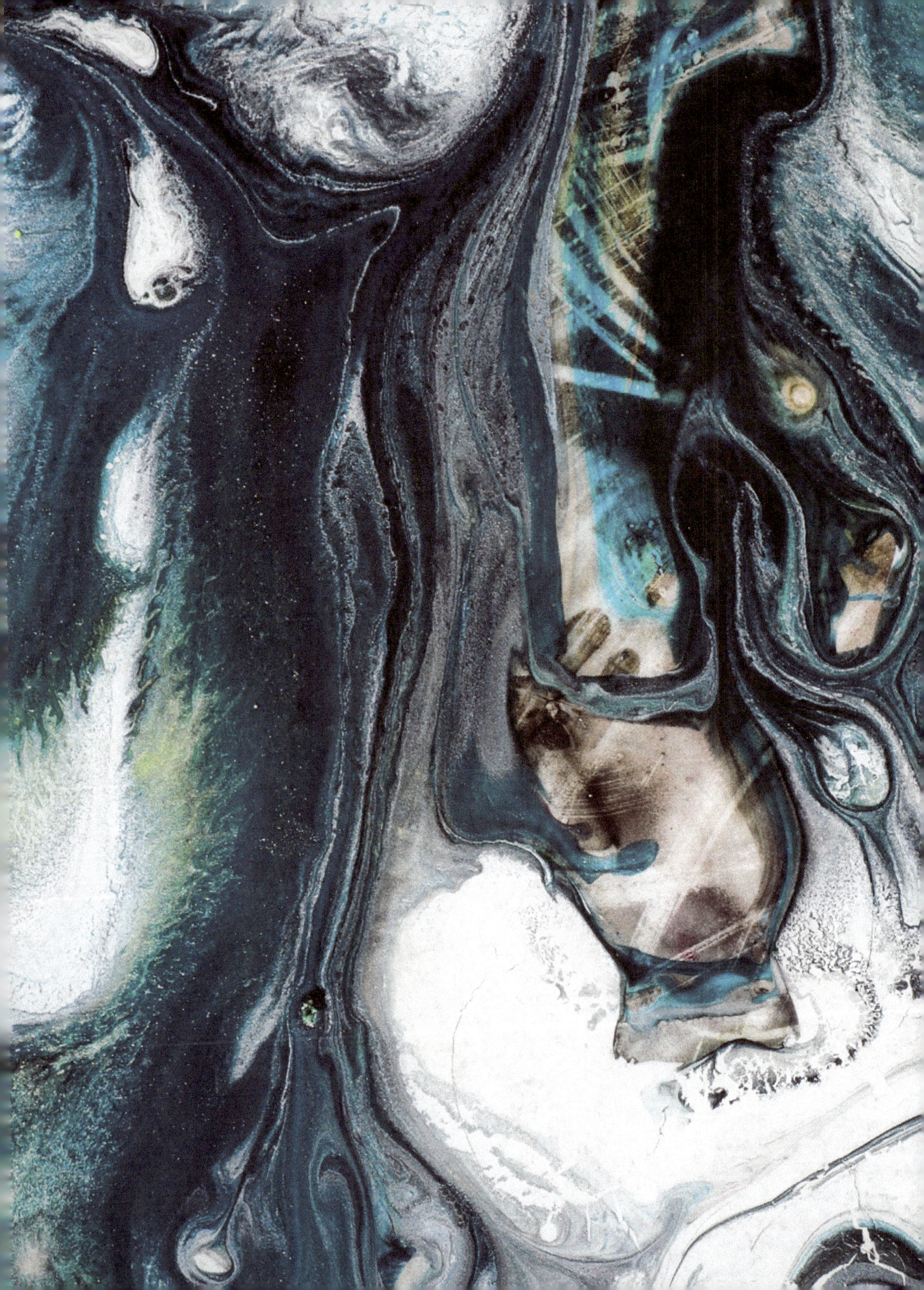

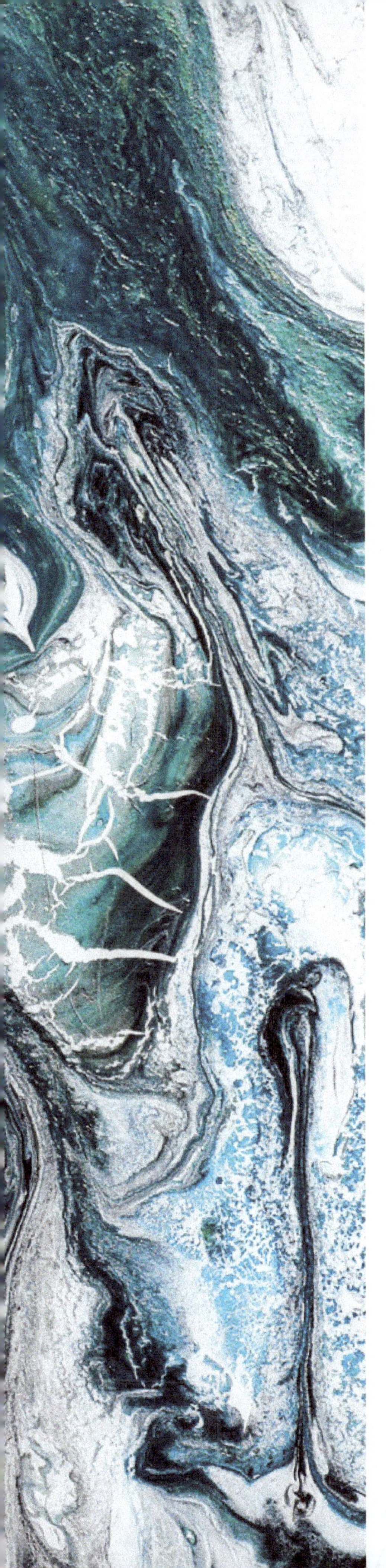

shine on edge. This can give you a better idea of how sharpened your blades are becoming befo- re you finish up with them, and it seems like a more practical way to sharpen several blades in one sitting. Still, the reviews seem to be equally as flattering as letting your machine do the work for you on one edge at a time.

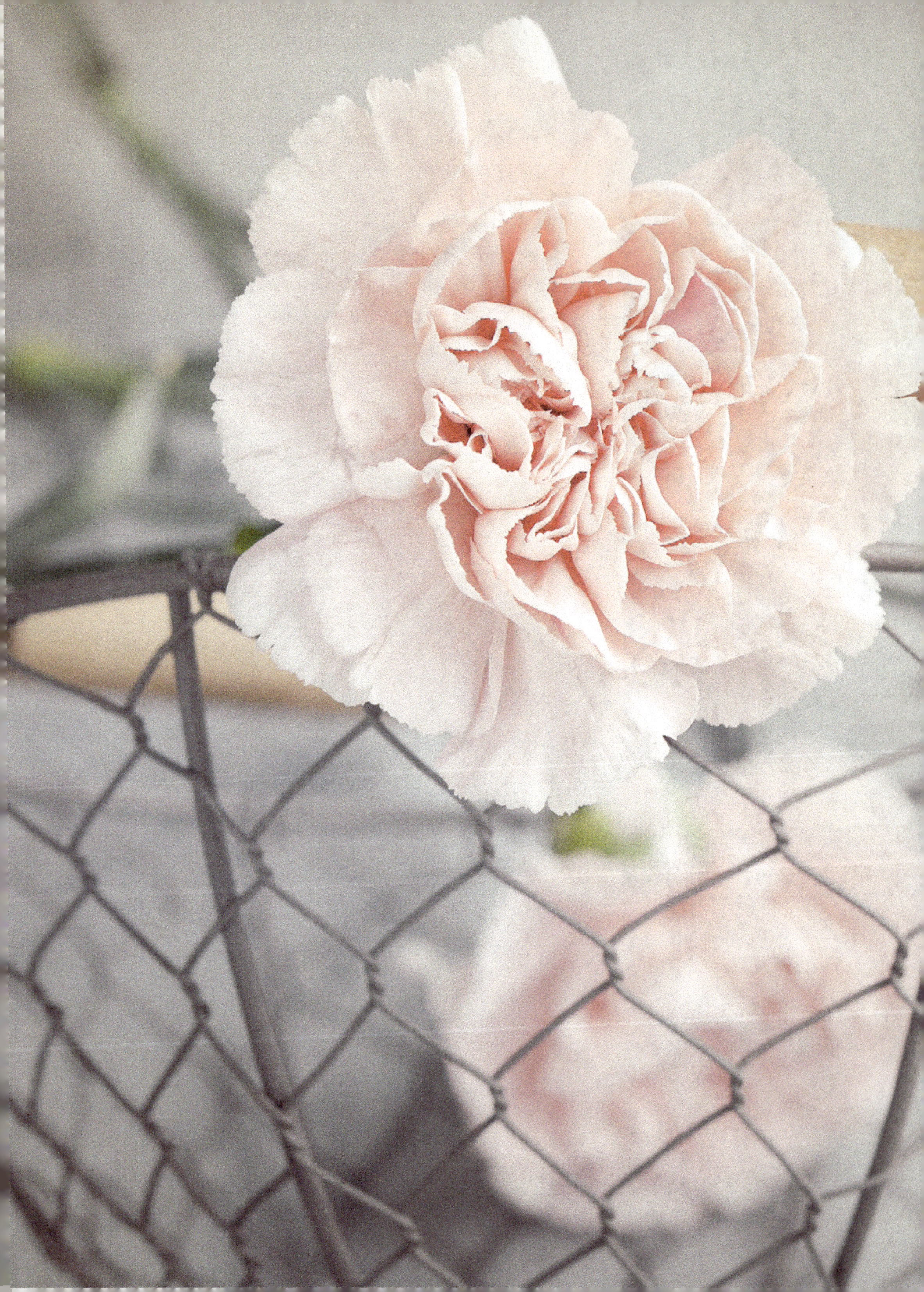

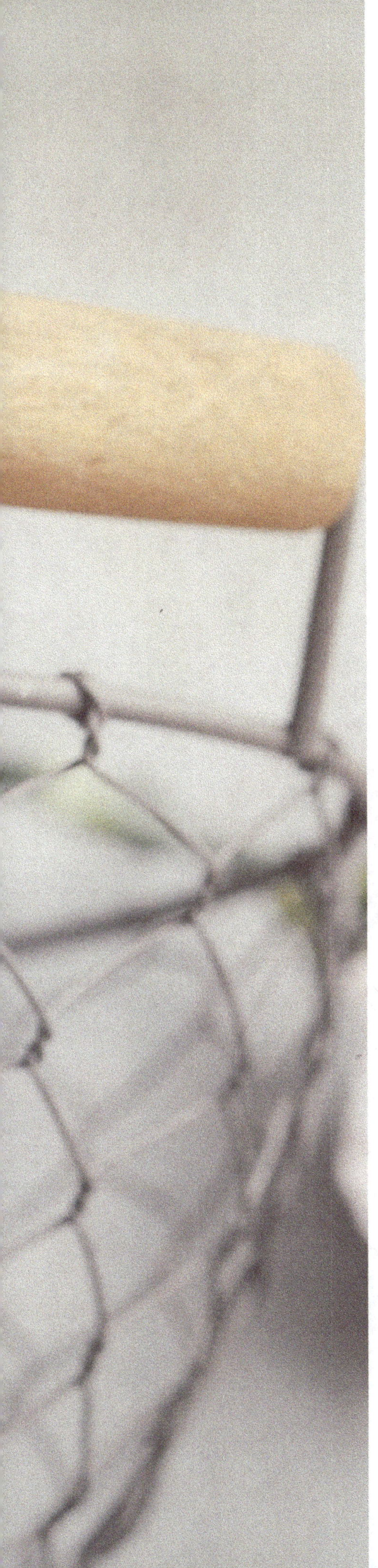

PAPER BOUQUET

Flowers are lovely, but it doesn't take long for them to wilt. How about some paper ones instead? They'll last you forever! Use this bouquet as décor in your home or for an event. Budget-conscious brides can even carry this down the aisle instead of an expensive floral arrangement! You will find plenty of templates in the Cricut Design Space for different flowers. You can also search online for more, or you can try your hand at making your own. A bouquet can be made up of one type of flower, the same height in different colors, a variety of flowers, or various flowers, all in the same color. It depends on the look and feels that you are going for, so use whatever method sounds best. You can use plain cardstock, patterned cardstock, or use watercolor to create a color gradient you love. For the stems, pipe cleaners are easier to work with and can be covered with tissue paper or something similar. Or it can be left visible for a crafty look. The floral wire will give a more realistic look, but it's thinner and takes some work.

SUPPLIES NEEDED

- Cardstock

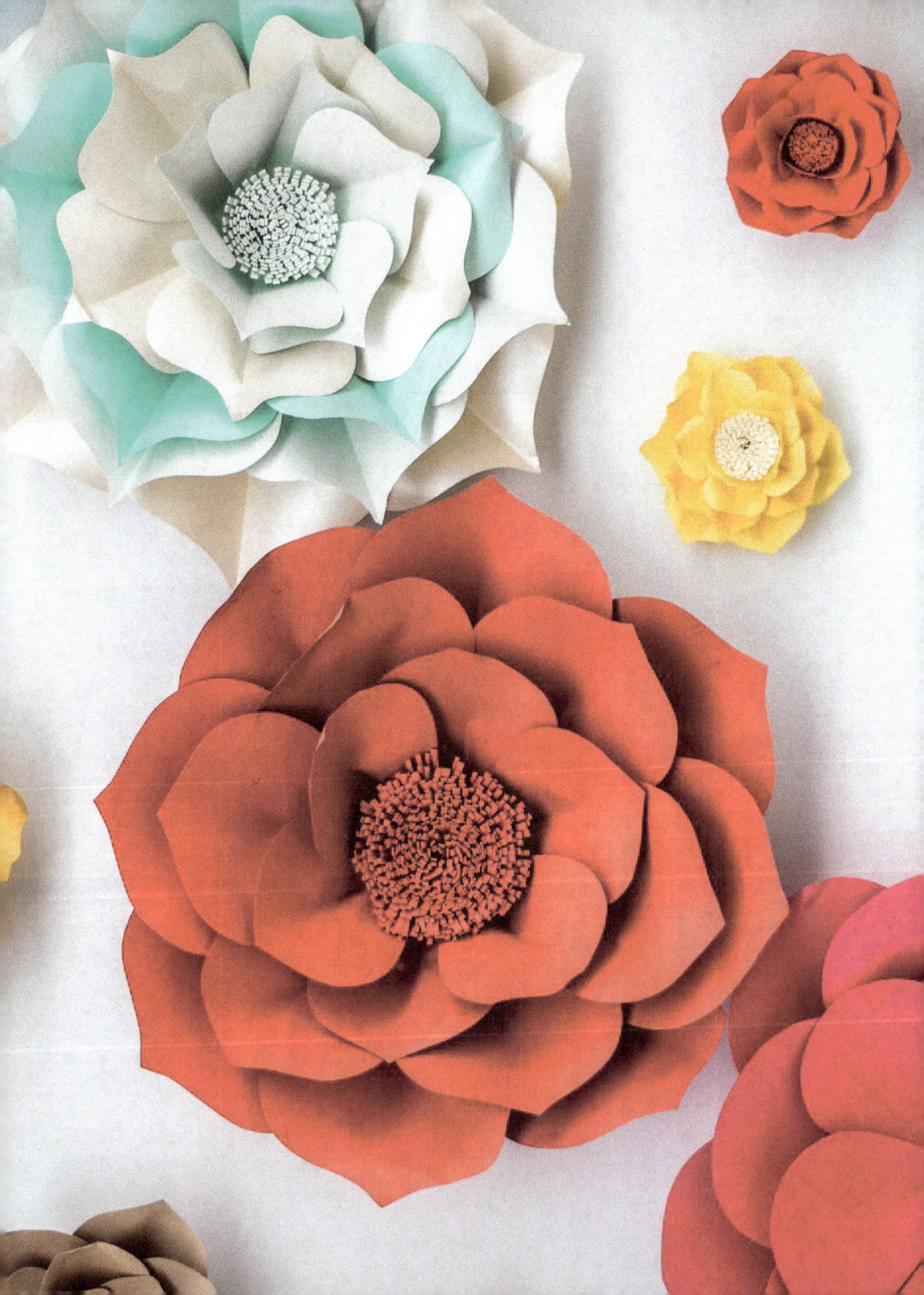

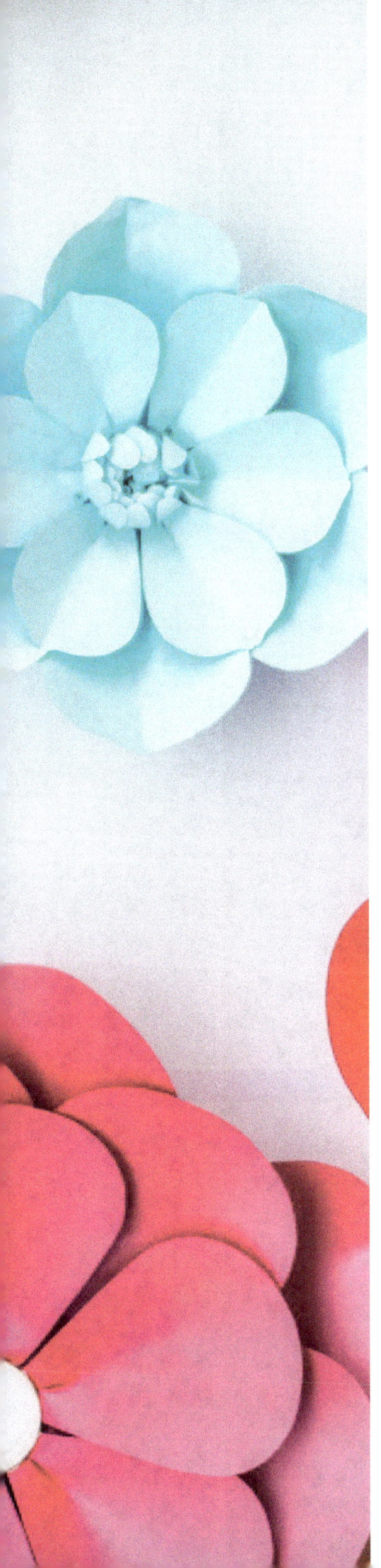

- Glue gun
- Lightstick cutting mat
- Weeding tool or pick
- Green pipe cleaners or floral wire

DIRECTIONS:

1. Open Cricut Design Space and create a new project.

2. Select the "Image" button in the lower left-hand corner and search for "paper flowers."

3. Select the image with several flower pieces and click "Insert."

4. Copy the flowers and resize them for variety in your bouquet.

5. Place your cardstock on the cutting mat.

6. Send the design to your Cricut.

7. Remove the outer edge of the paper, leaving the flowers on the mat.

8. Use your wedding tool or carefully pick to remove the flowers from the mat.

9. Glue the flower pieces together in the centers, with the largest petals at the bottom.

10. Bend or curl petals as desired to create multiple looks.

11. Glue the flowers to the ends of the pipe
cleaners or sections of floral wire.

12. Gather your flowers together in a vase or wrap
them with tissue paper.

13. Enjoy your beautiful bouquet!

LEAFY GARLAND

Garlands are an easy way to spruce up any space, and there is an infinite variety of them. Create a unique leafy one to give your home a more naturalistic feel! Feel free to change the leaves' colors to suit you, whether you stick with green or go a little more unnatural. Tweaking the size of the bundles you make and how close you put them together will change the garland's look. You can use different types of leaves as well. Experiment a little bit to see what you like best. Bending the plates down the center and curling the edges a little will give you a more realistic look, or you can leave them flat for a handmade look.

SUPPLIES NEEDED

- Cardstock - 2 or more colors of green or white to paint yourself
- Glue gun
- Lightstick cutting mat
- Weeding tool or pick
- Floral wire
- Floral tape

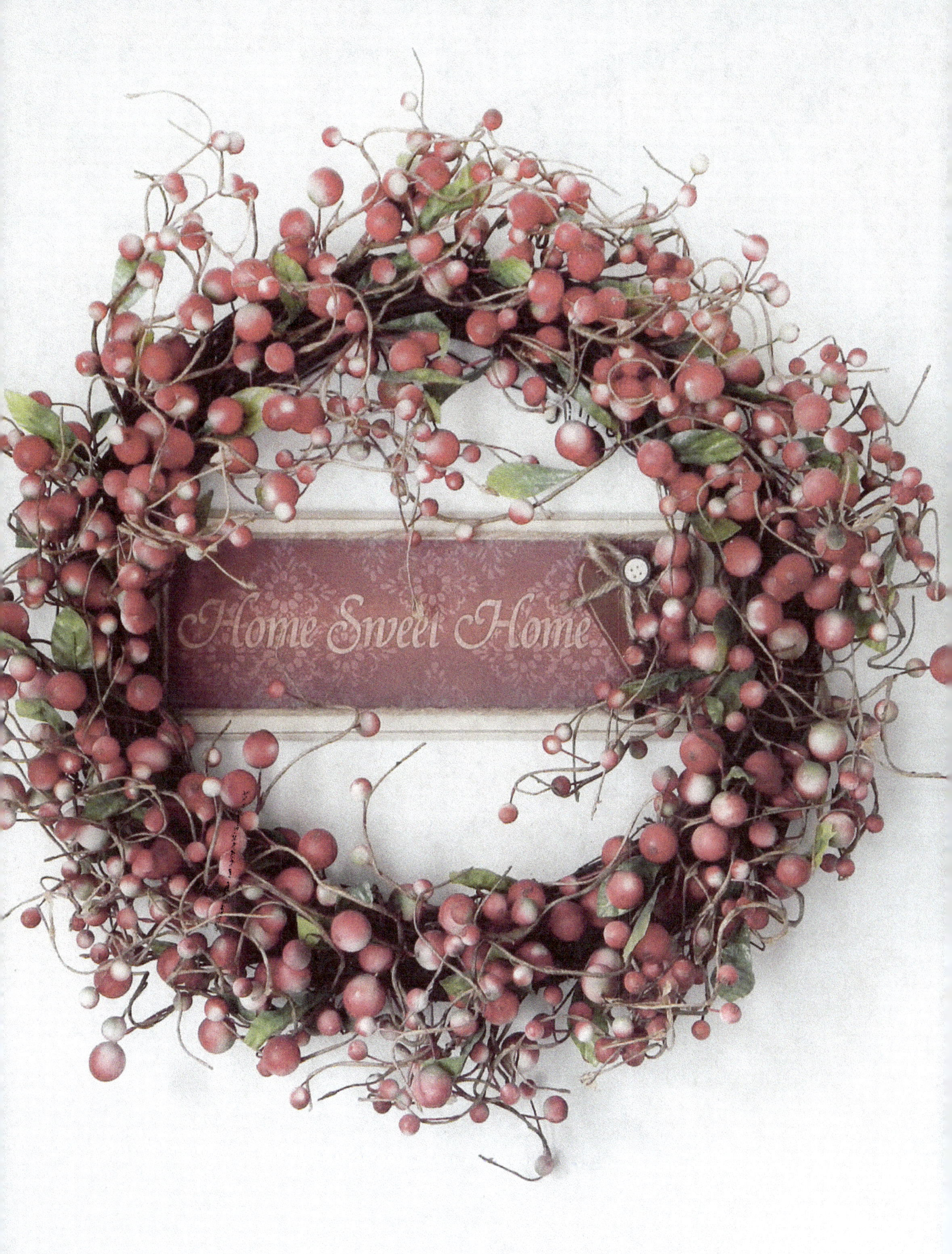

Home Sweet Home

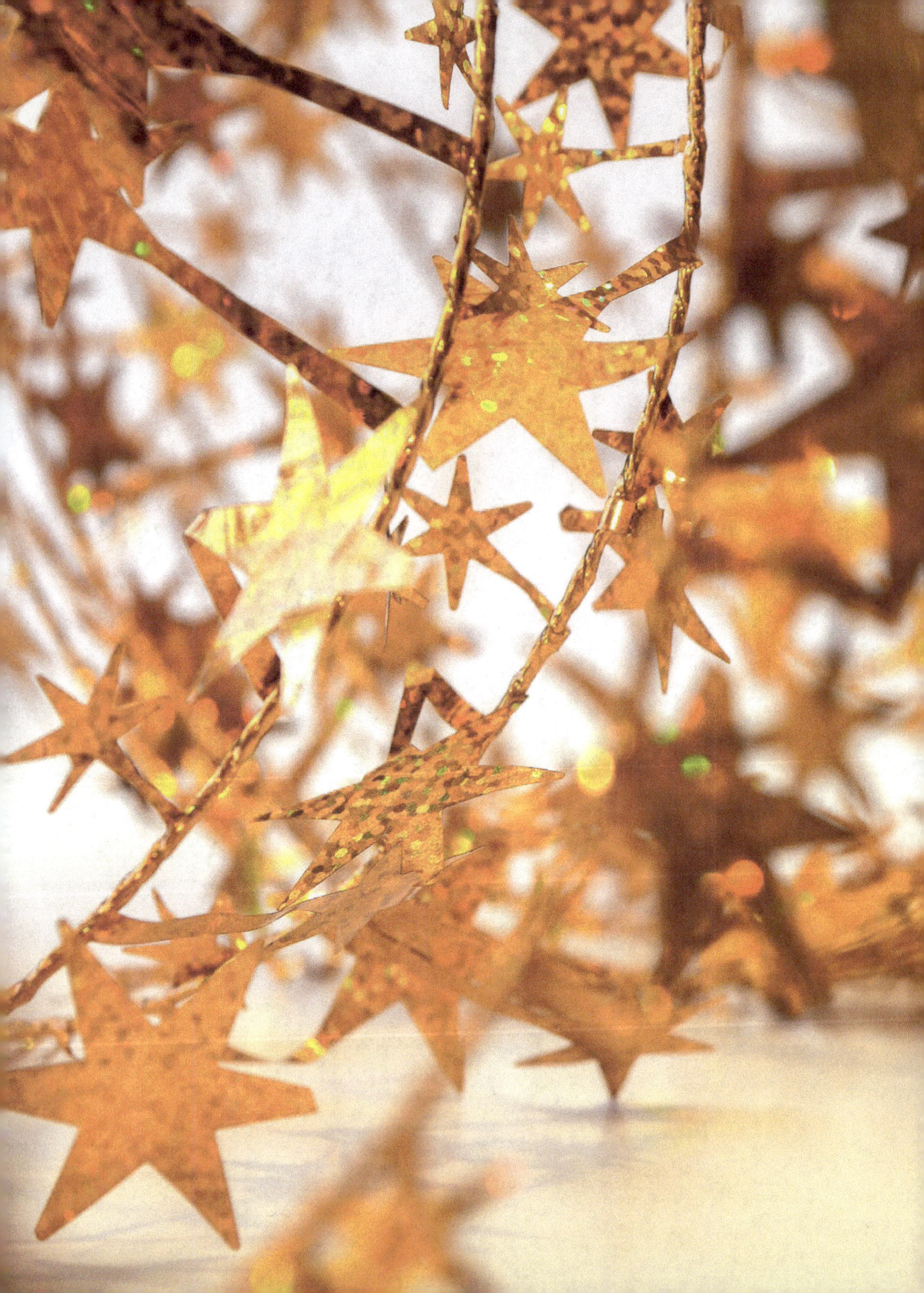

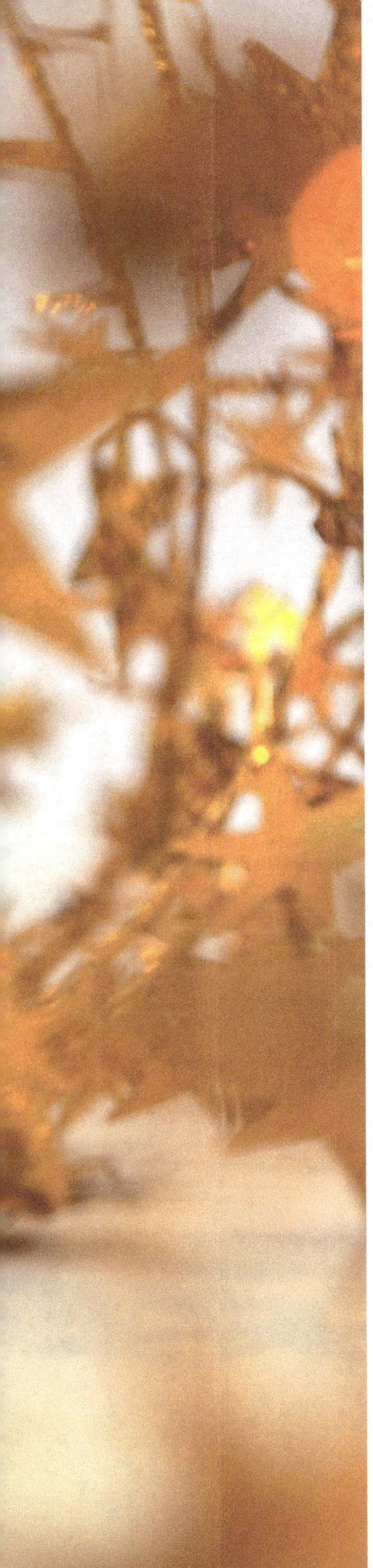

DIRECTIONS:

1. Open Cricut Design Space and create a new project.

2. Select the "Image" button in the lower left-hand corner and search for "leaf collage."

3. Select the image of leaves and click "Insert."

4. Place your cardstock on the cutting mat.

5. Send the design to your Cricut.

6. Remove the outer edge of the paper, leaving the leaves on the mat.

7. Use a pick or scoring tool to score down the center of each leaf lightly.

8. Use your wedding tool or carefully pick to remove the leaves from the mat.

9. Gently bend each leaf at the scoreline.

10. Glue the leaves into bunches of two or three.

11. Cut a length of floral wire to your desired garland size, and wrap the ends with floral tape.

12. Attach the leaf bunches to the wire using floral tape.

13. Continue attaching leaves until you have a garland of the size you want. Bundle lots of plates

for a full look, or spread them out to be sparser.

14. Create hooks at the ends of the garland with
    floral wire.

15. Hang your beautiful leaf garland wherever you'd
    like!

EASY ENVELOPE ADDRESSING

Christmas cards are lovely to send out, but they can take forever to address. Address labels just don't look as personal, though. Use the Cricut pen tool in your machine to "hand letter" your envelopes! You can use this for your batch of holiday cards or even for other cards or letters. This takes advantage of the writing function of your Cricut machine. For the most realistic written look, make sure you select a font in the writing style. It will still write other fonts, but it will only create an outline of them, a different look you could go for! Cricut offers a variety of Pen Tools, and some other pens will fit as well. Addressing envelopes, stick to black or another color that is easy to read so that the mail makes it to its destination.

SUPPLIES NEEDED

- Envelopes to address
- Cricut Pen Tool

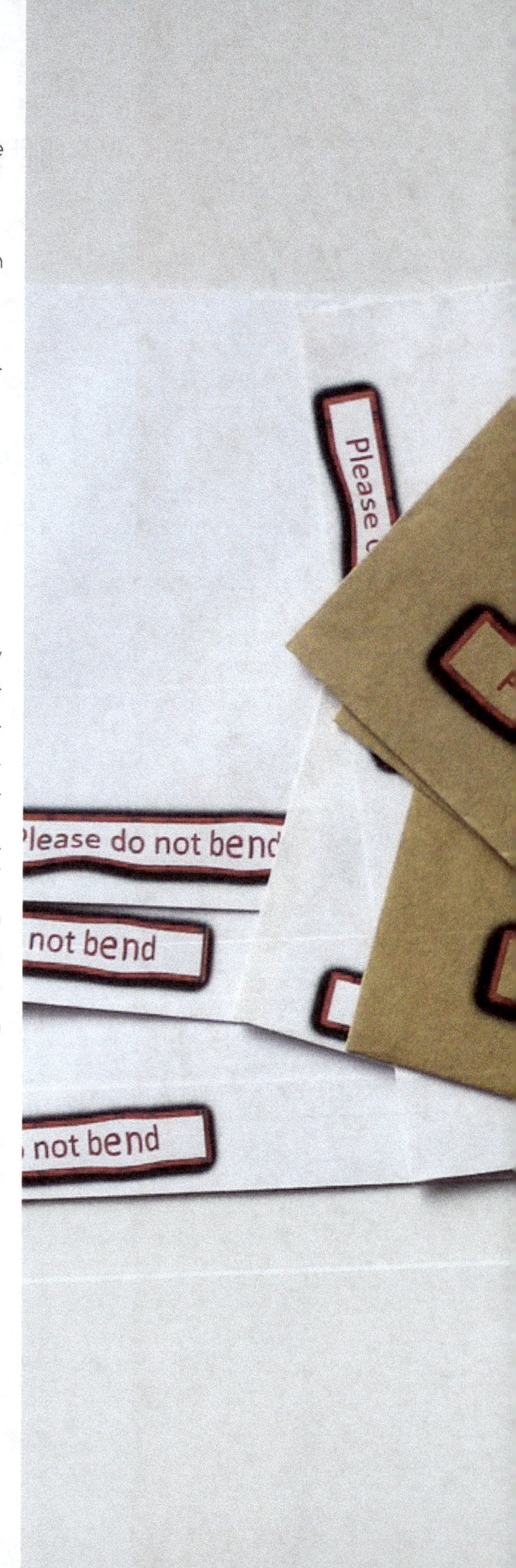

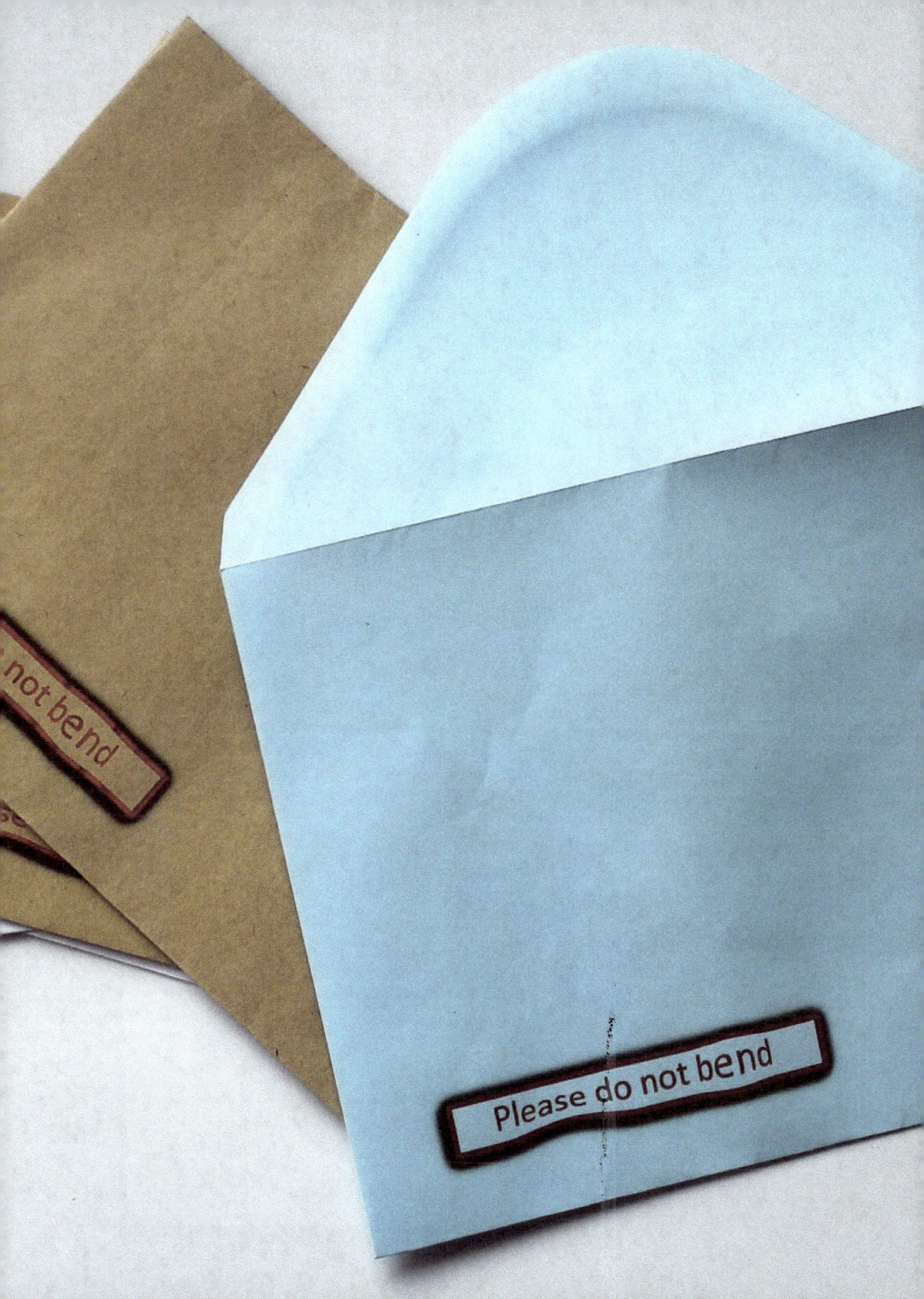

not bend
Please do not bend

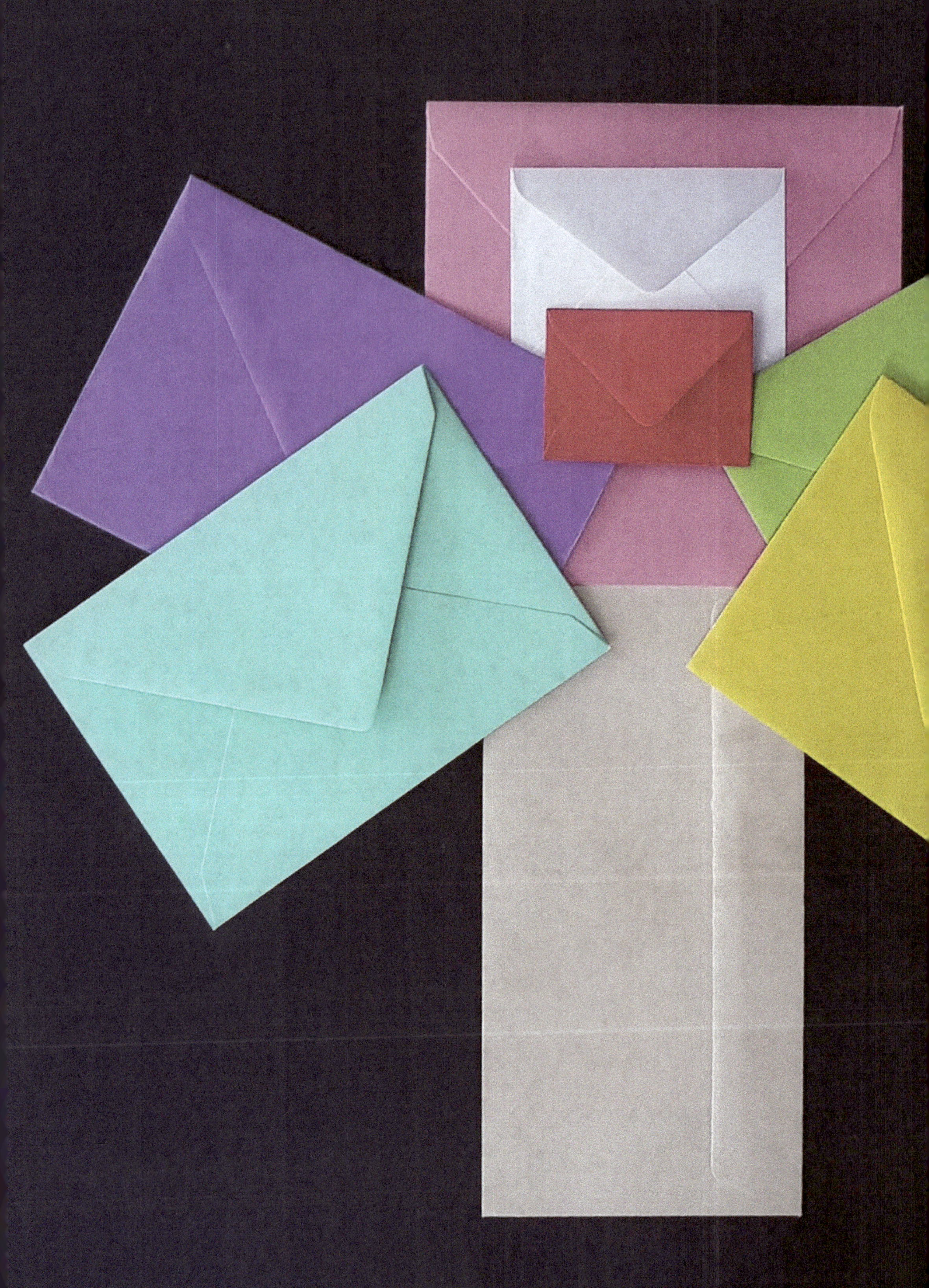

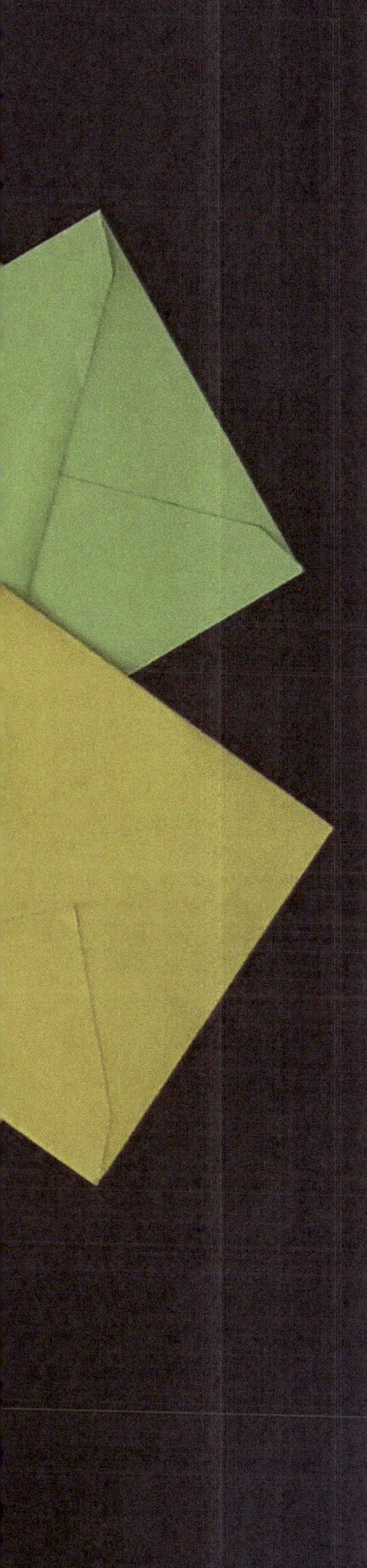

- Lightstick cutting mat

DIRECTIONS:

1. Open Cricut Design Space and create a new project.

2. Create a box of the appropriate size for your envelopes.

3. Select the "Text" button in the lower left-hand corner.

4. Choose one handwriting font for a uniform look or different fonts for each line to mix it up.

5. Type your return address in the upper left-hand corner of the design.

6. Type the "to" address in the center of the design.

7. Insert your Cricut pen into the auxiliary holder of your Cricut, making sure it is secure.

8. Place your cardstock on the cutting mat.

9. Send the design to your Cricut.

10. Remove your envelope and repeat as needed.

11. Send out your "hand-lettered" envelopes!

WOODEN GIFT TAGS

Dress up your gifts with unique wooden tags! Balsa wood is light and easy to cut. The wood tags with gold names will give all of your skills a shabby chic charm. Change up the vinyl color as you see fit; you can even use different colors for different gift recipients. People will be able to keep these tags and use them for something else, as well. An alternative to balsa wood is chipboard, though it won't have the same look.

SUPPLIES NEEDED

- Balsa wood
- Gold vinyl
- Vinyl transfer tape
- Cutting mat
- Weeding tool or pick

DIRECTIONS

Secure your small balsa wood pieces to the cutting mat, then tape the edges with masking tape for additional strength.

Open Cricut Design Space and create a new project.

Select the shape you would like for your tags and set the Cricut to cut wood, then send the design to the Cricut.

Remove your wood tags from the Cricut and remove any excess wood.

In Cricut Design Space, select the "Text" button in the

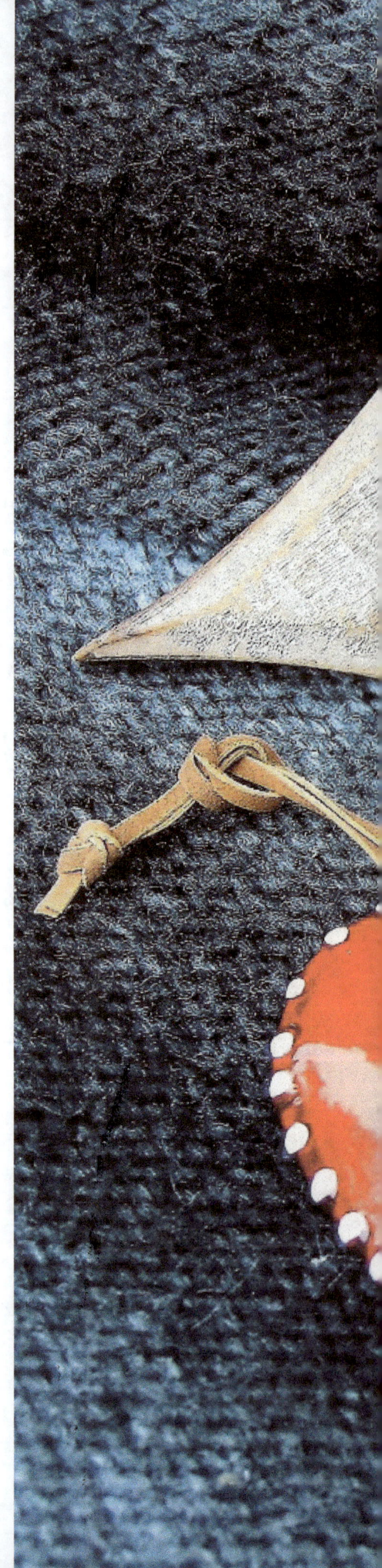

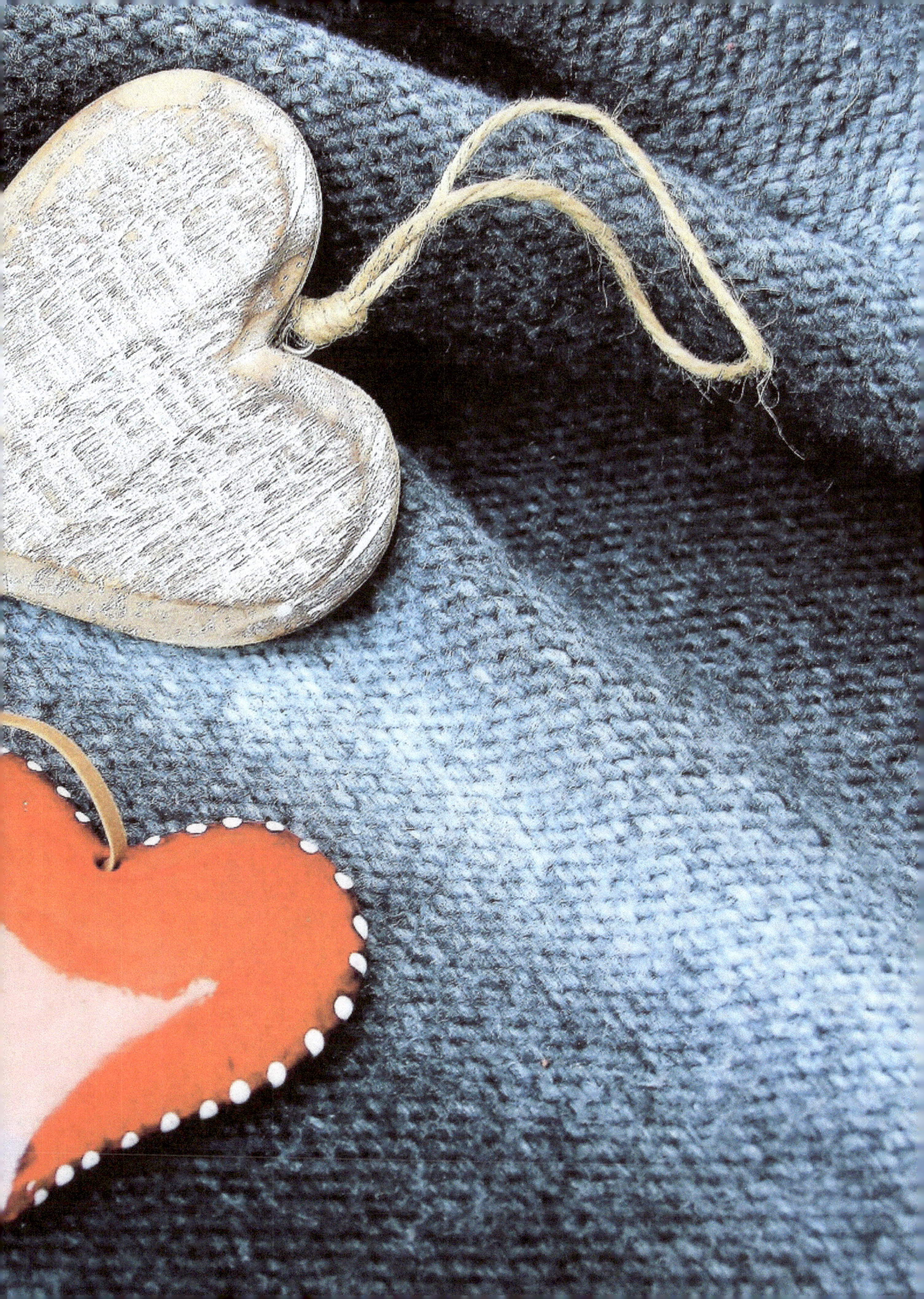

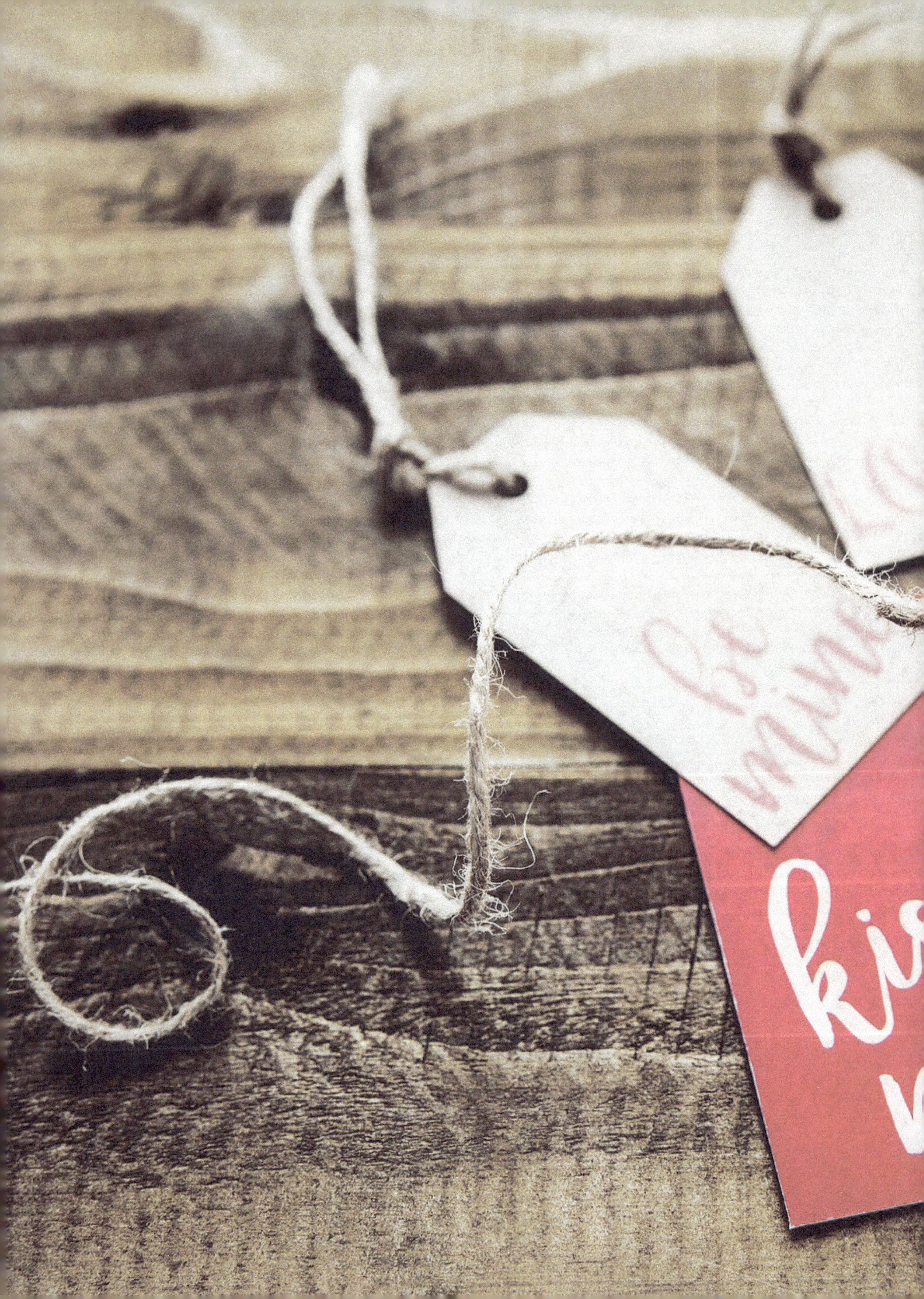
be mine
kiss

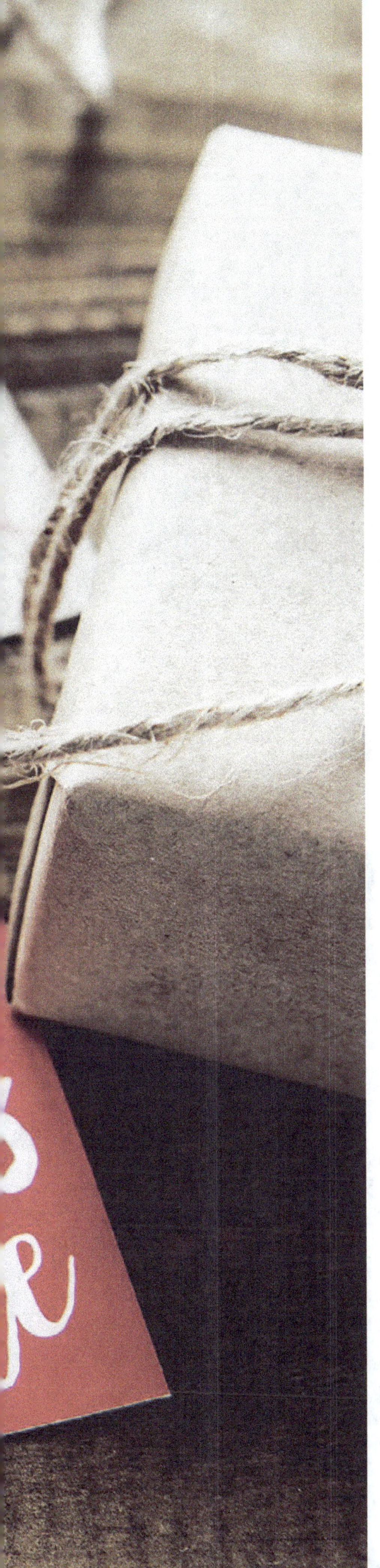

lower left-hand corner.

Choose your favorite font, and type the names you want to place on your gift tags.

Place your vinyl on the cutting mat.

Send the design to your Cricut.

Use a weeding tool or pick to remove the excess vinyl from the text.

Apply transfer tape to the quote.

Remove the paper backing from the tape.

Place the names on the wood tags.

Rub the tape to transfer the vinyl to the wood, making sure there are no bubbles. Carefully peel the tape away.

Thread twine or string through the holes, and decorate your gifts!

PET MUG

Show your love for your pet every morning when you have your coffee! A cute silhouette of a cat or dog with some paw prints is a simple but classy design. You're not limited to those two animals, either. Use a bird with bird footprints, a fish with water drops, or whatever pet you might have! You can add your pet's name or a quote to the design as well. You have the freedom here to arrange the aspects of the design however you'd like. You could put the animal in the center surrounded by the paw prints, scatter the images all around the mug, place the animal next to its name and paw prints along the top, or whatever else you can imagine. Think of this as a tribute to your favorite pet or dedication to your favorite animal, and decorate accordingly.

SUPPLIES NEEDED

· Plain white mug
· Glitter vinyl
· Vinyl transfer tape
· Cutting mat
· Weeding tool or pick

DIRECTIONS:

Open Cricut Design Space and create a new project.

Select the 'Image' button in the lower left-hand corner and search for 'cat,' 'dog,' or any other pet of your choice.

Choose your favorite image and click 'Insert.'

Search images again for paw prints, and insert them into your design.

Arrange the pet and paw prints how you'd like them on the mug.

Place your vinyl on the cutting mat.

Send the design to your Cricut.

Use a weeding tool or pick to remove the excess vinyl from the design.

Apply transfer tape to the design.

Remove the paper backing, and apply the design to the mug.

Rub the tape to transfer the vinyl to the mug, making sure there are no bubbles. Carefully peel the tape away.

Enjoy your custom pet mug!

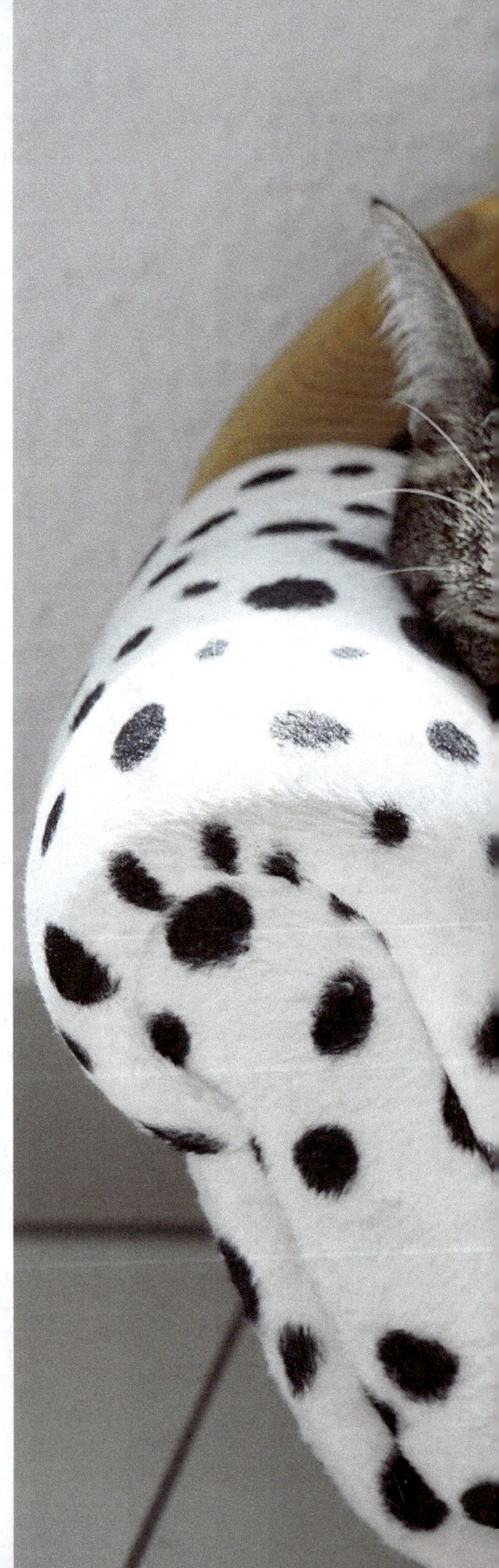

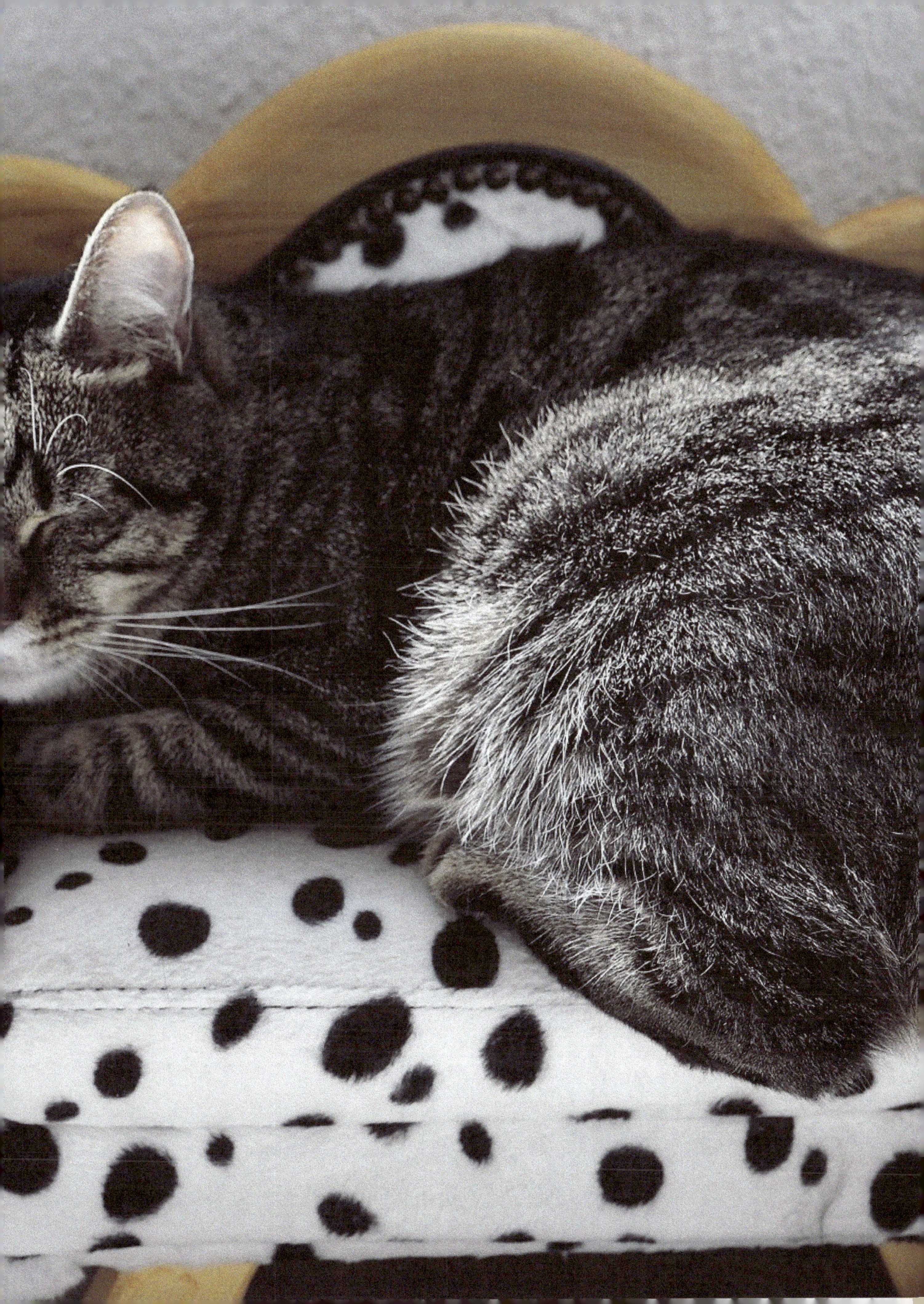

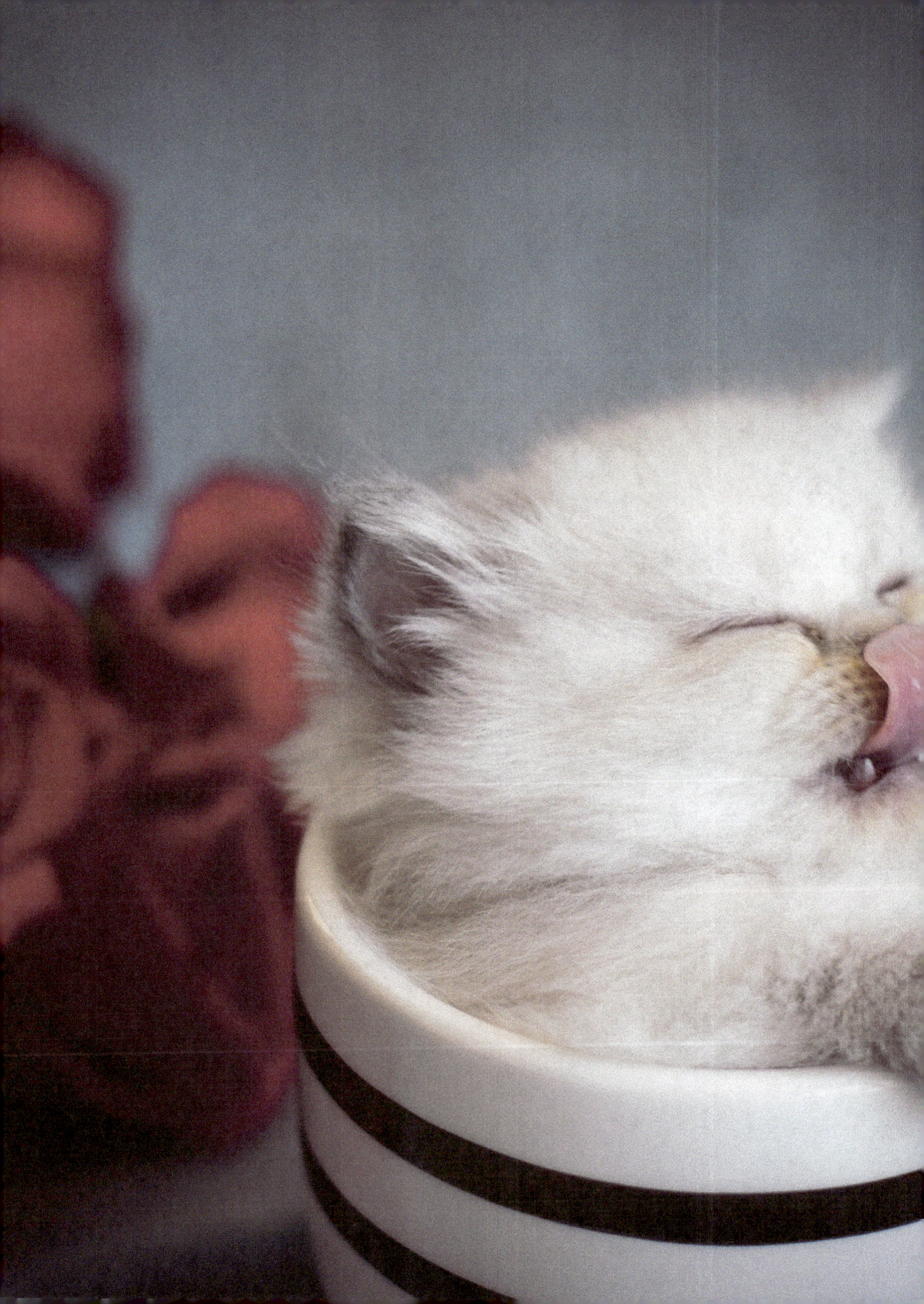

ROSE GOLD LEATHER EARRINGS DIY

With a Cricut Maker, you can do so many incredible things! Some honeymoon earrings only take a few minutes to make. The leather earrings are perfect because they can be enormous, but they are lightweight and comfortable. These golden roses are great! Make a fast pair of earrings for a gift, wear, and fun, and make a bunch for sale!

SUPPLIES NEEDED:

- Cricut Maker
- Cricut Strong Grip Mat
- Clear Contact Paper
- Cricut Metalic Rose Gold Vinyl
- Cricut tools
- Hook and jump rings
- Cricut Metal leather Gold Cricut

DIRECTIONS:

Start by stitching a clear contact paper to the backside of the leather. This keeps everything from the matt surface and keeps the mat more useful. Place the leather on the strong grip mat (contact paper side down).

To design a rope shape with a tiny hole cut at the top, use Cricut Design Space. Cut it off, then. I shouted. I was using the blade for the knife, but I was too tired to switch to it. And the leather wasn't cut all around its rear edge, so there's a bit of fluff. I cut it off

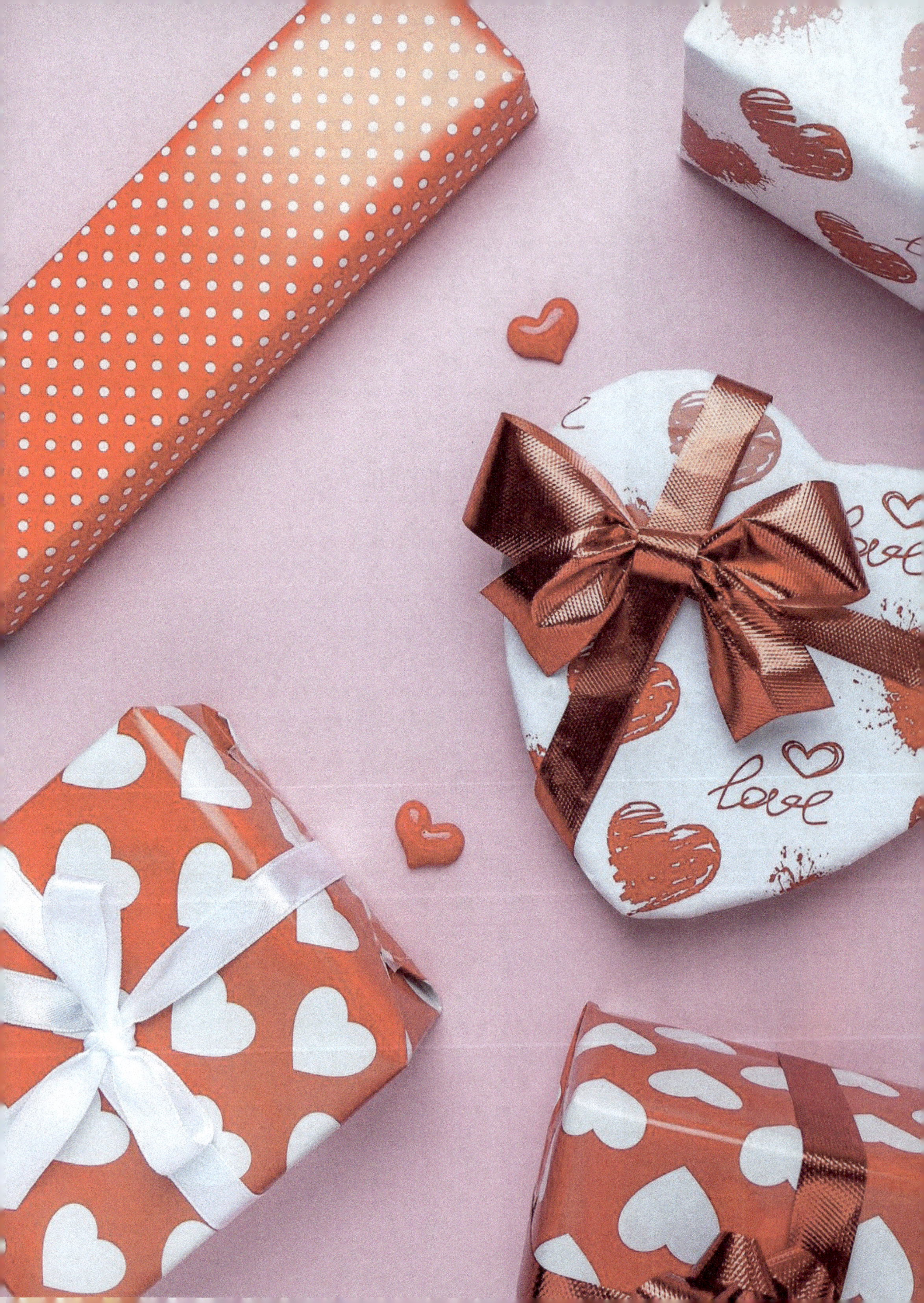

with the scissors of Cricut.
Then use some pins to attach a hook to the leather earring.
Cut some sweet shapes out of metallic rose vinyl gold. These are the forms in the Cricut Access file I found on a CDS.
Then peel the leather and stick it to the back. The rose-gold and rose-gold vinyl go hand in hand.
Under the layers of leather, I like the hit metallic.
Such a simple DIY on an excellent declaration pair of earrings
The lobby and collect one supply!

VALENTINE'S DAY CLASSROOM CARDS

SUPPLIES:

Cricut Maker Card Designs (Write Stuff Coloring)
Cricut Design Space Dual Scoring Wheel Pens
Cardstock Crayons Shimmer Paper

INSTRUCTIONS

1. Open the Card Designs (Write Stuff Coloring) on the Design Space, and then click on "Make it" or "Customize" to make edits.

2. When all the changes have been done, Cricut will request you to select a material. Select Cardstock for the Cards and Shimmer Paper for the Envelopes.

3. Cricut will send you a notification when you need to change the pen colors while creating the Card, and then it will start carving the Card out automatically.

4. You will be prompted later on to change the blade because of the Double Scoring Wheel. It is advisable to use the Double Scoring Wheel with Shimmer Paper; they both work best together.

5. When the scoring has been finished, replace the Scoring Wheel with the last blade.

6. After that, fold the flaps at the Score lines in the direction of the paper's white side, and then attach the Side Tabs to the Bottom Tab's exterior by gluing them together.

7. You may now write "From:" and "To:" before placing the Crayons into the Slots.

8. Place the Cards inside the Envelopes and tag them with a sharp object.

GOLD FOIL ROSE IRONON VINYL ON CRICUT STRAW BAG!

SUPPLIES NEEDED:

- Cricut EasyPress 2
- Cricut EasyPress
- Rose Gold Foil Iron-on Vinyl
- Cricut Maker

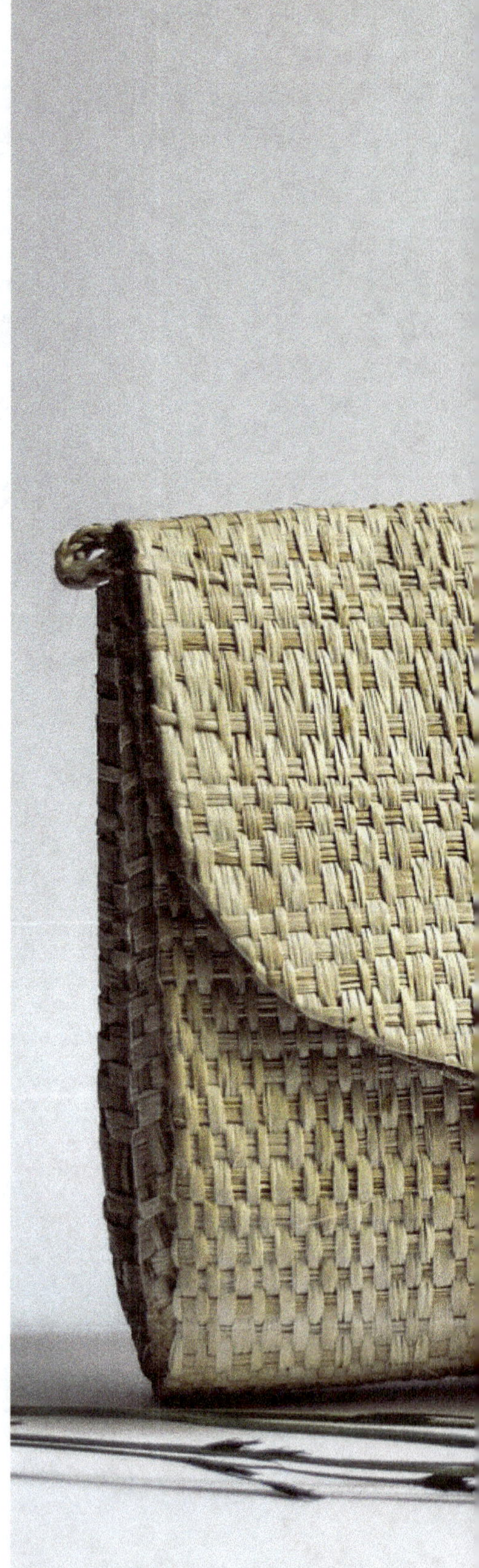

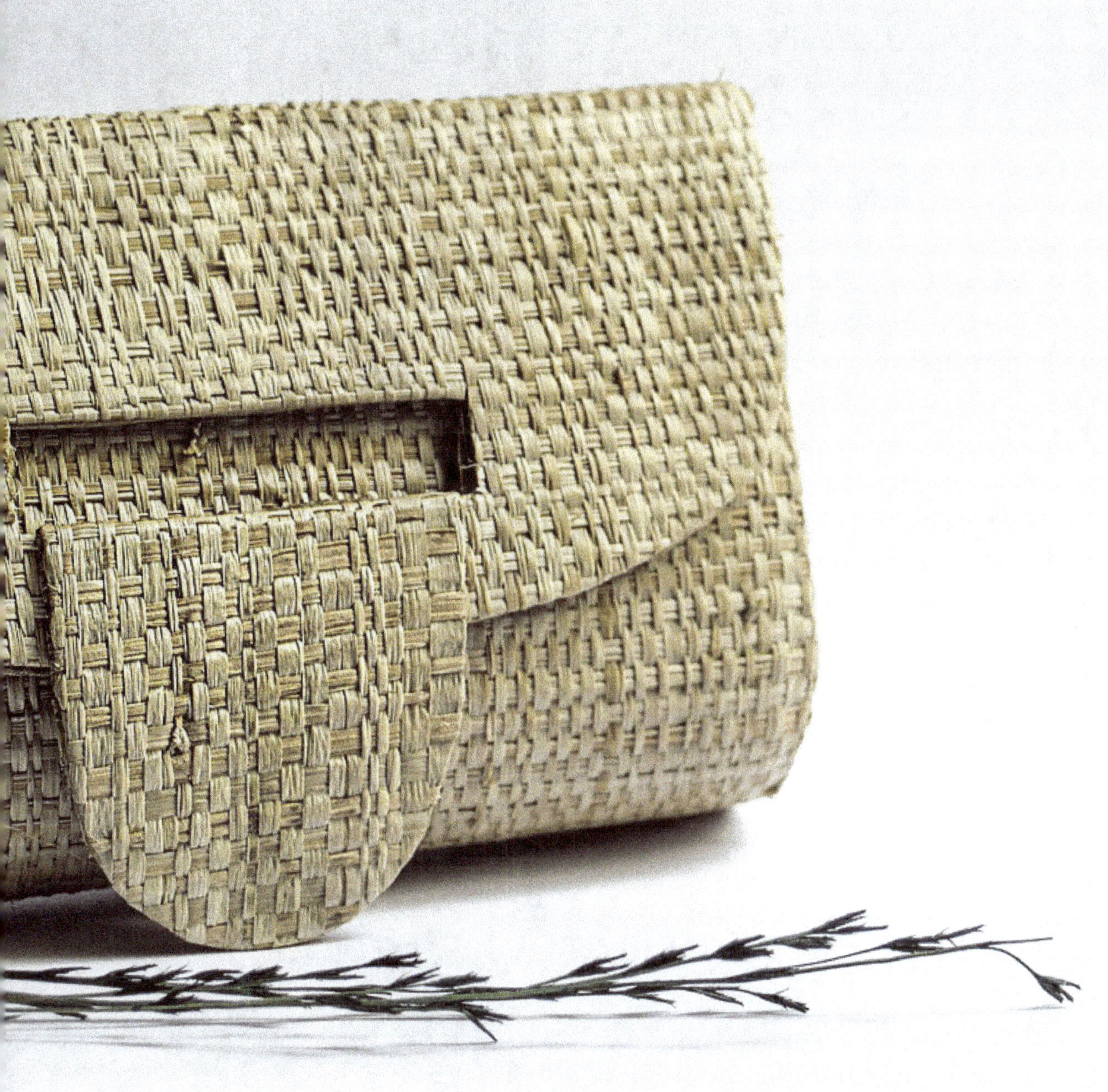

- Cricut EasyPress Mat

INSTRUCTIONS:

Set it on the top of the bag with a bright side. Remain firm while it presses inside the bag with towels.
Cover with a cover or Teflon board to prevent the melting of the bag.
Set the EasyPress 2 at the correct material temperature. Pull down firmly while heating (Check this chart).
Let the project entirely refresh before the carrier plate is removed.
The bag is now ready to be gifted or filled!

PERSONALIZED MUGS (IRON-ON VINYL)

SUPPLIES NEEDED

- Cricut Maker
- standard grip mat,
- "Cricut" iron-on or heat transfer vinyl
- "Cricut Easy Press Mini"
- "Easy Press" mat
- weeding tool
- ceramic mug

INSTRUCTIONS:

Login to "Design Space" using your "Cricut" ID and click on "New Project" to view a blank Canvas

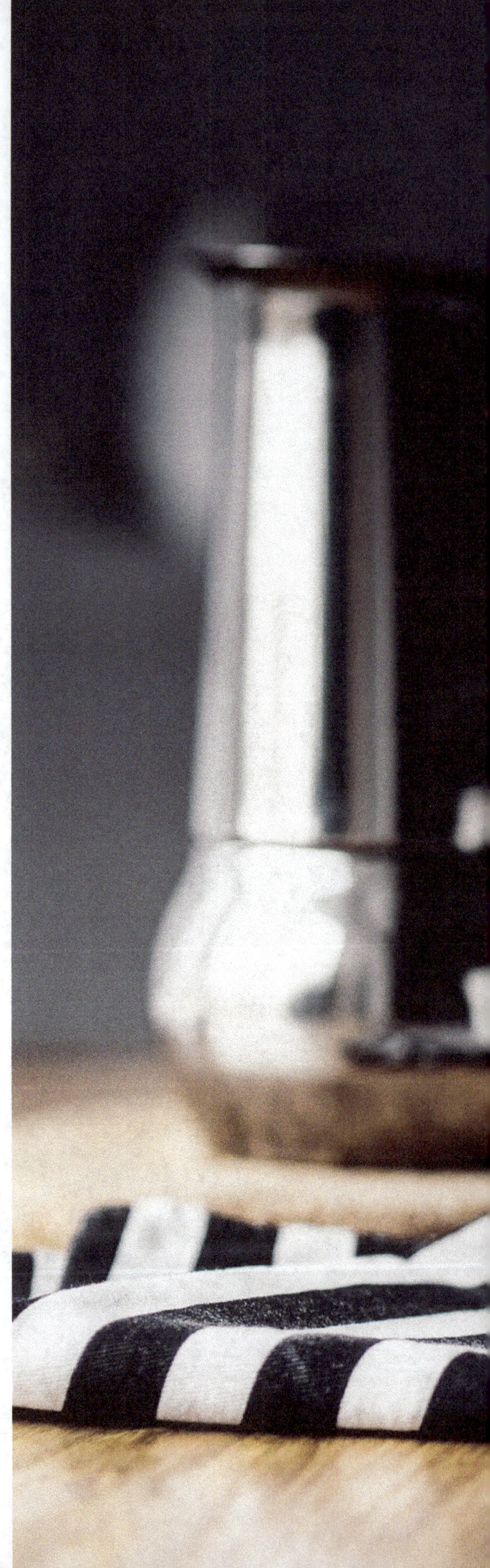

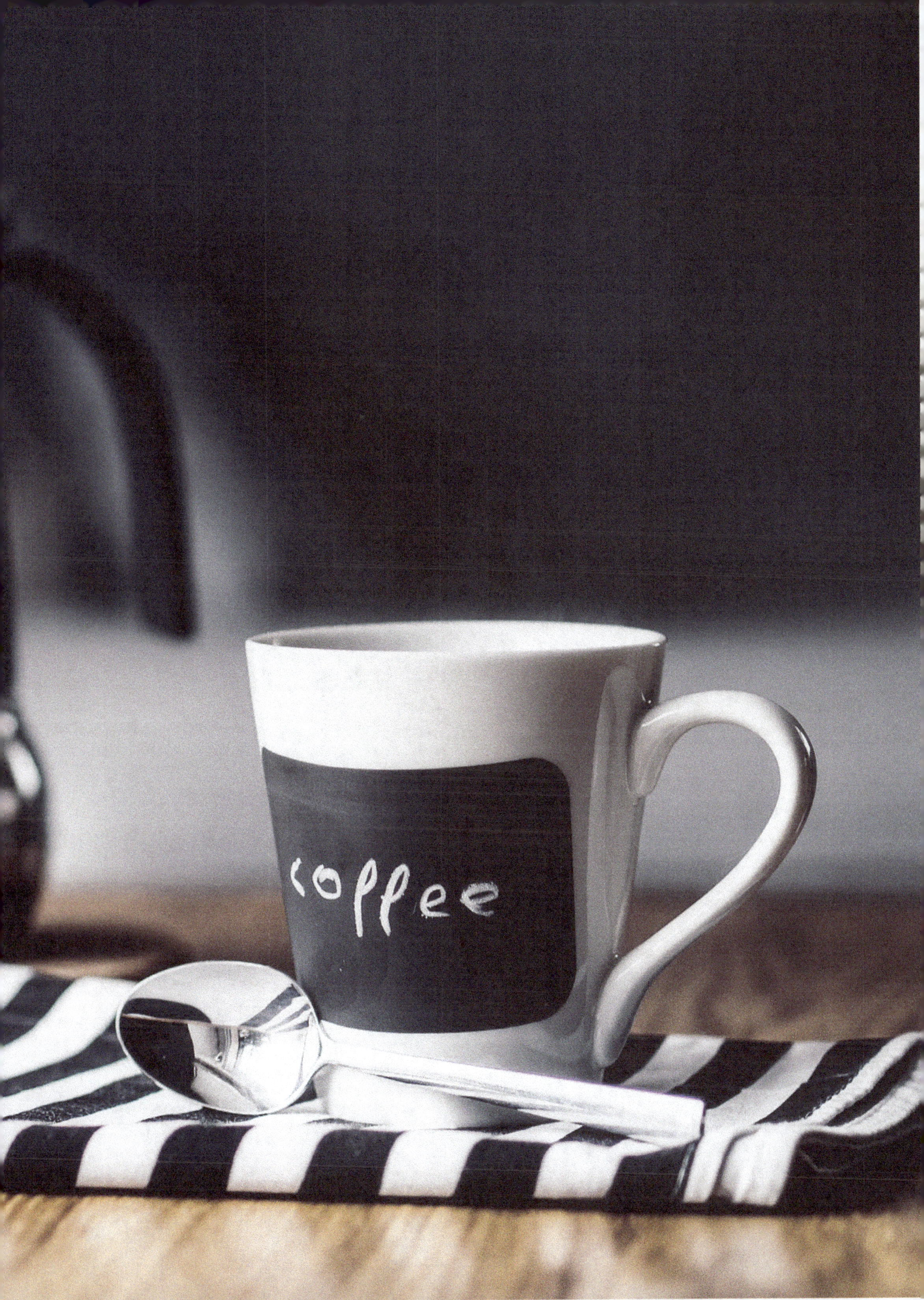

coffee

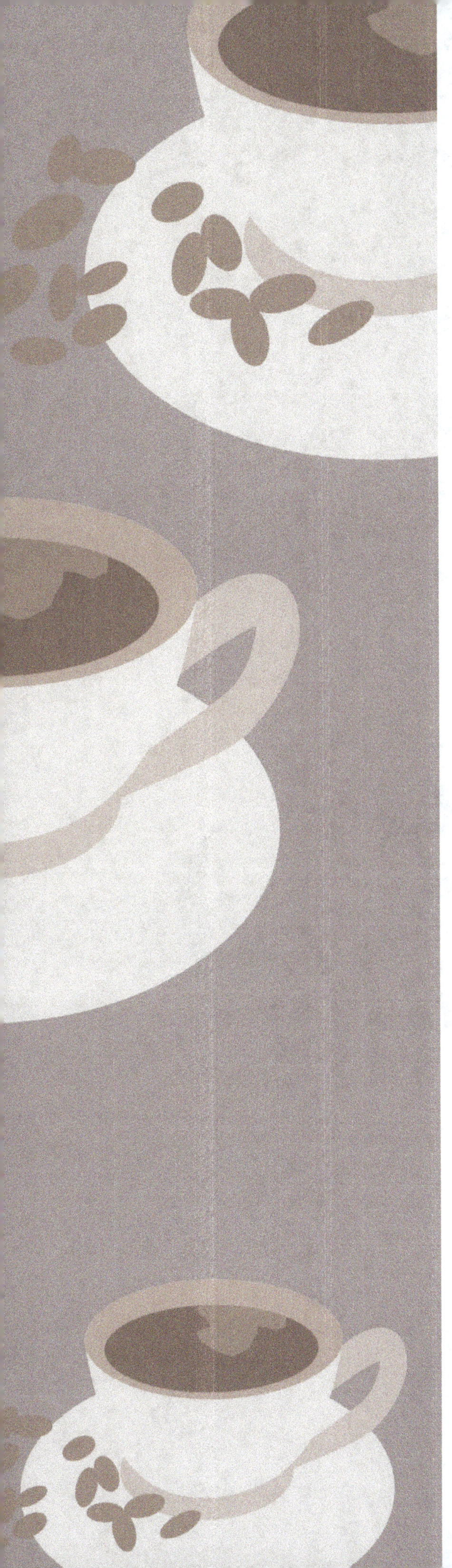

Click on the "Images" icon on the "Design Panel" and type in "America" in the search bar to narrow your search. Select the image that you like, then click on "Insert Images" at the bottom of the screen, as shown in the picture below.

Your selected images will appear on the Canvas, as shown in the picture below. Click on the "Templates" icon, "Designs Panel" on the left of the screen, and type in "mug" in the templates search bar to quickly find the mug template for your project, as shown in the picture below.

Click on the mug icon, and you will see the mug template loaded on the Canvas with your selected design picture, as shown in the image below.

Now click on the "mugs" icon at the bottom right of the screen, and you will see the options to change the "Type" and "Size" of the template if you have a non-standard si- zed mug. Click on the "Size" icon and select "Custom" to enter your mug size. Click on the "Lock" icon if your mug size needs to be adjusted further. You can also select your mug's color to make your design even more compatible with your actual cup, as shown in the picture below.

You can now edit your image as needed; for example, you could resize the image to fit in on the mug template. Click on the "Shapes" icon on the "Designs Panel" if you would like to add hearts, stars, or other shapes to your design in desired shape and color to customi-

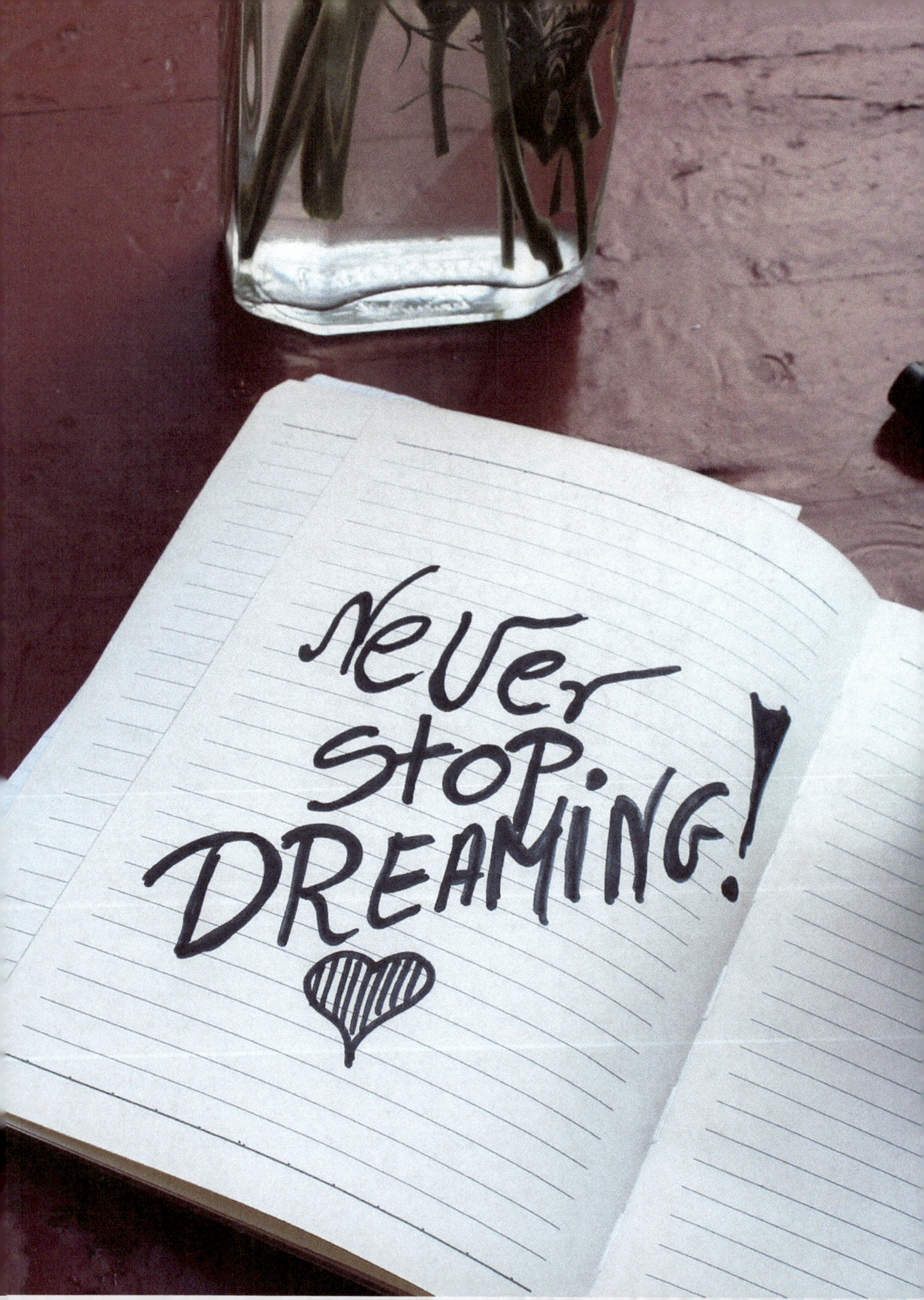
NeVer
stop.
DReaMinG!

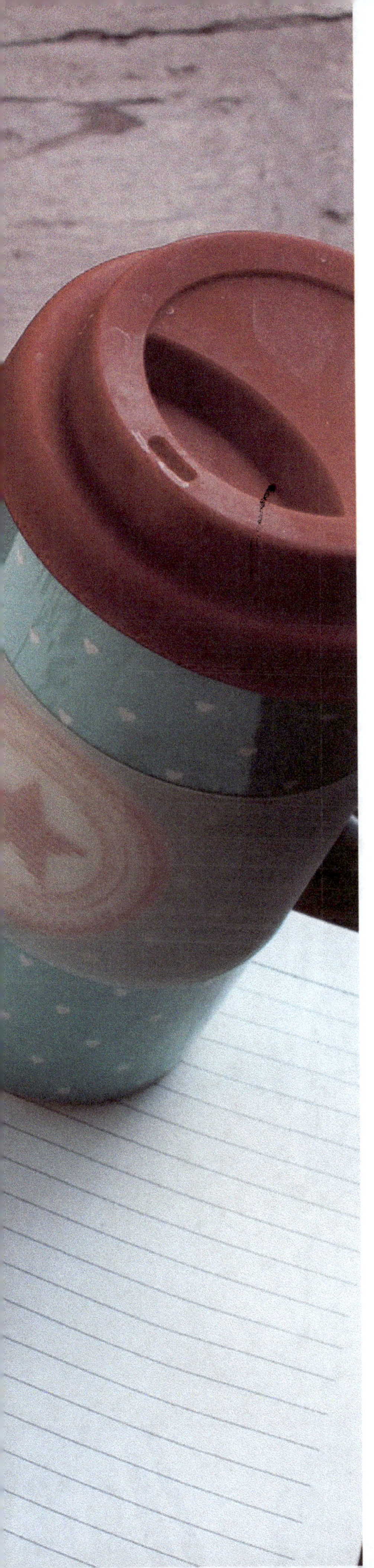

ze it further, as shown in the picture below.

Click on "Save" at the top right corner of the screen and give the desired name to the project, for example, "Mug Decoration," and click "Save."

Simply click on the "Make It" button on the top right corner of the screen. You will see the required mats and material displayed on the screen. Make sure you click on the "Mirror" button under the "Material Size" on the screen's left and as shown in the picture below.

Click "Continue" at the bottom right corner of the screen. Load the iron-on material to the "Cricut" machine and print the design.

Note - The images used are available for purchase, so click on "Purchase" at the bottom right of the screen to buy the photos before you can print them. And once you have made the purchase, the "Continue" button will be available to you.

Calibrate the machine with your device and use the appropriate setting to cut your chosen material. Place the iron-on with its shiny side (clear liner) down on the cutting mat. Load your mat into your "Cricut" machine, and "Design Space" will guide you through cutting the image. Carefully remove the excess material from the sheet using the "weeder tool," making sure only the design remains on the clear liner.

Using the "Cricut Easy Press Mini" and "Easy Press Mat," the iron-on layers can be easily transferred to your mug. Preheat your "Easy Press Mini," and put your design on the desired area and apply pressure for a couple of minutes or more (Sample project in the picture below). Wait for few minutes before peeling off the design while it is still warm. (Since the procedure is delicate, use the spatula tool or your fingers to rub the letters down the mug before starting to peel the design). You now have a personalized profile to flaunt your love of Washington DC!

CLEAR PARTY FAVOR BOXES

SUPPLIES NEEDED

- Cricut Maker'
- standard grip mat
- scoring wheel
- foil acetate

INSTRUCTIONS:

Login to "Design Space" using your "Cricut" ID and click on "New Project" to view a blank Canvas Again, we will use an already existing project from the "Cricut" library and customize it since it's the most straightforward approach for beginners to get their hands-on experience without having a lot of prior practice. So, click on the "Projects" icon on the "Design Panel" and click on the "All Categories" drop-down menu to view all existing projects that you can select from. For this example, we will click on "Parties & Events" then type in "favor box" in the search bar to narrow your search to party favor box projects, as shown in the picture below.

You can view all the projects available by clicking on them, and a pop-up window displaying all the details of the project will appear on your screen. The project selected for this example is shown in the picture below.

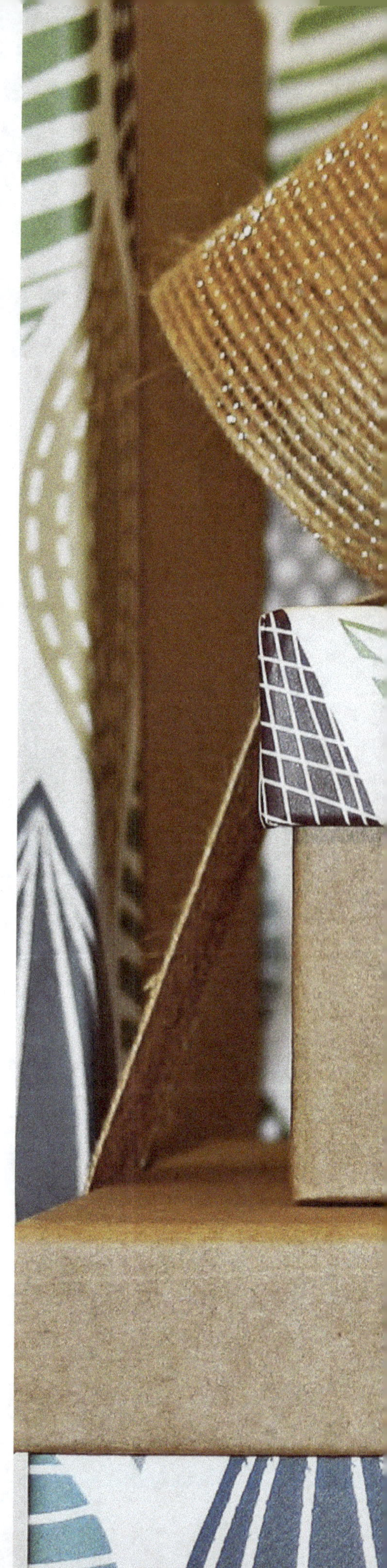

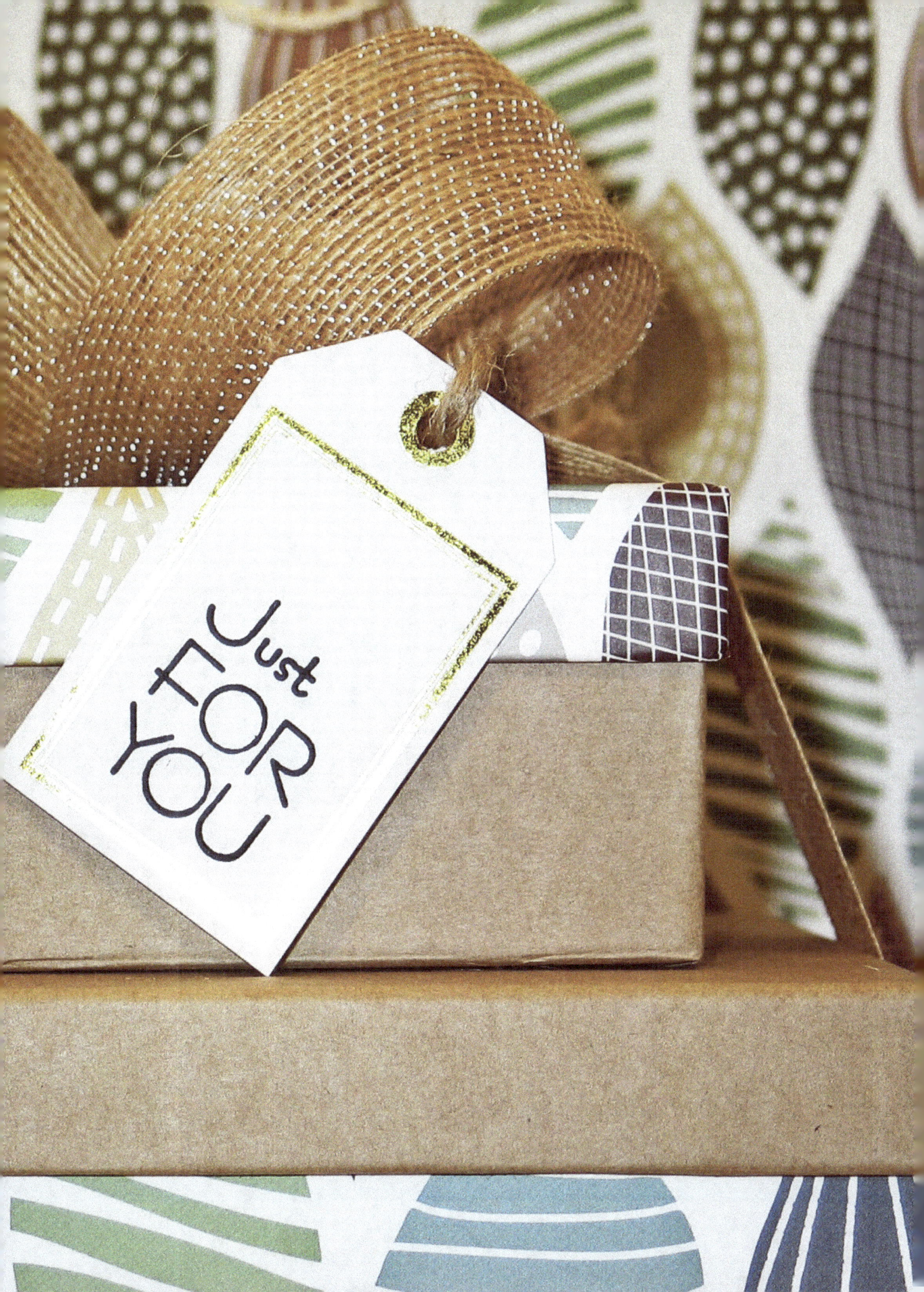

Just
FOR
YOU

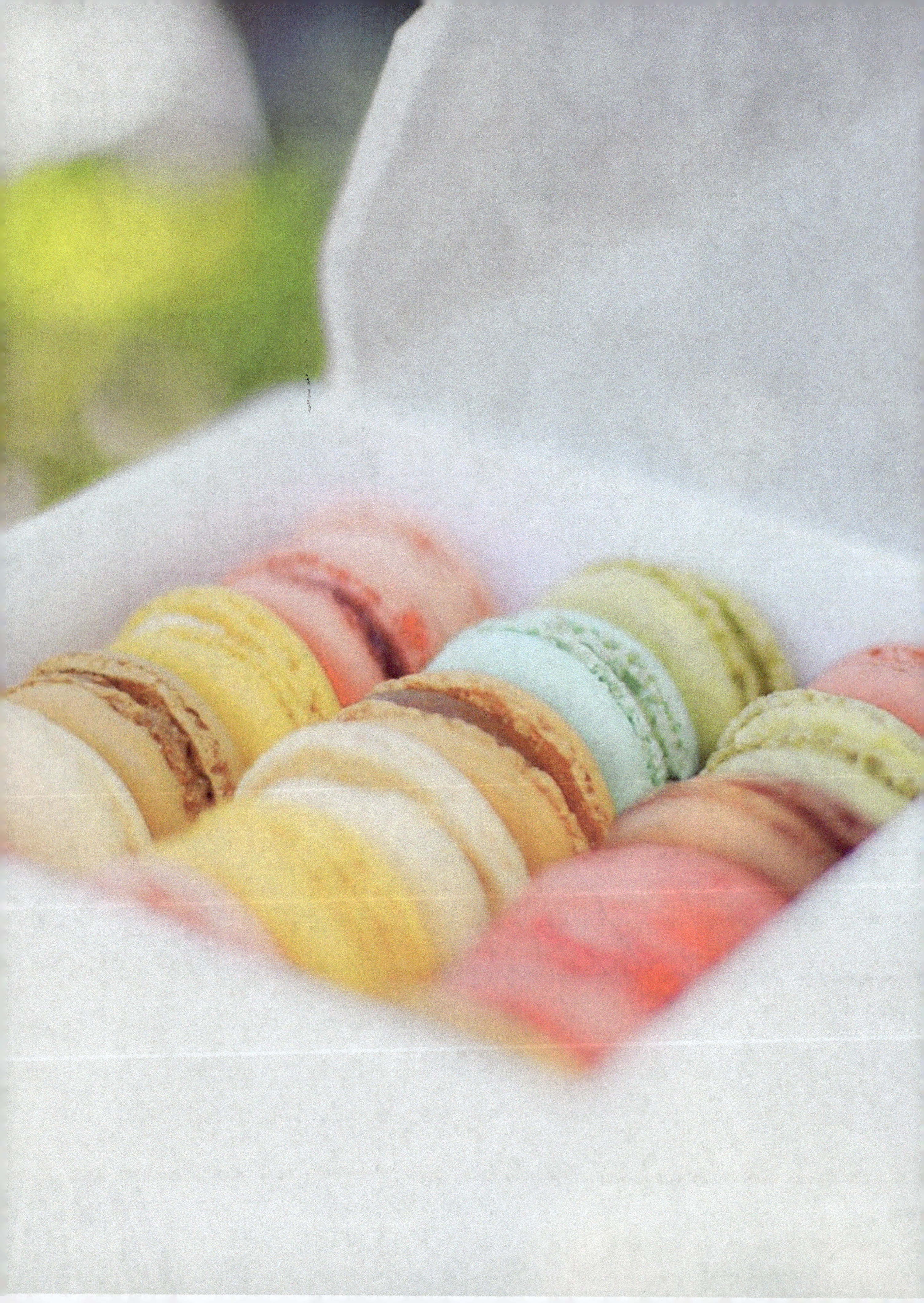

Click on "Customize" so you can edit the project to your preference. Remember when you change the size of the design, i.e., the box, change the grouped design simultaneously, and do not attempt to resize a particular piece so you would not end up with a plan that doesn't fit together upon folding.

Now, your design is ready to be scored and cut. Simply click on the "Make It" button on the top right corner of the screen. You will see the required mats and material displayed on the screen. Set the material to "Foil Acetate" and mount the scoring wheel. Make sure you click on the "Mirror" button under the "Material Size" on the left of the screen. Click "Continue" at the bottom right corner of the screen after you have loaded the vinyl to the "Cricut" machine and print the design onto the paper. Note - The image used is available for purchase, so click on "Purchase" at the bottom right of the screen to buy the pictures before you can print them. And once you have made the purchase, the "Continue" button will be available to you.

Place the foil acetate on the mat with the shiny or the pretty side down. Calibrate the machine with your device and use the appropriate setting to cut your chosen material. Place the vinyl on top of the cutting mat and load it into the "Cricut" machine by pushing against the rollers. The "Load/Unload" button will start flashing, so just press it. Then press the "Go" button, which would already be flashing.

Once the scoring has been completed, replace the scoring wheel with the fine point blade to finish the design's cutting. Press the "Go" button again, which would already be flashing.

After you have unloaded the mat, carefully remove the foil from the carpet and fold the box along the score lines and push the triangle tabs into the available slots around the whole package. The final product would look as shown in the picture below. Fill your boxes with candy or other goodies, and you have your personally designed party favors!

TRICK OR TREAT BAG

SUPPLIES NEEDED

*   "Cricut Maker"
*   standard grip mat
*   transfer tape
*   scraper
*   everyday vinyl
*   small kraft paper bags

INSTRUCTIONS:

Login to "Design Space" using your "Cricut" ID and click on "New Project" to view a blank Canvas Click on the "Images" icon on the "Design Panel" and type in "Halloween" in the search bar to narrow your search for the images used in the project. Select any other idea that may catch your eye and click on "Insert Images" at the screen's bottom.

Your selected images will appear on the Canvas. You can notice from the "Layers Panel" on the right that one of the pictures has multiple layers,

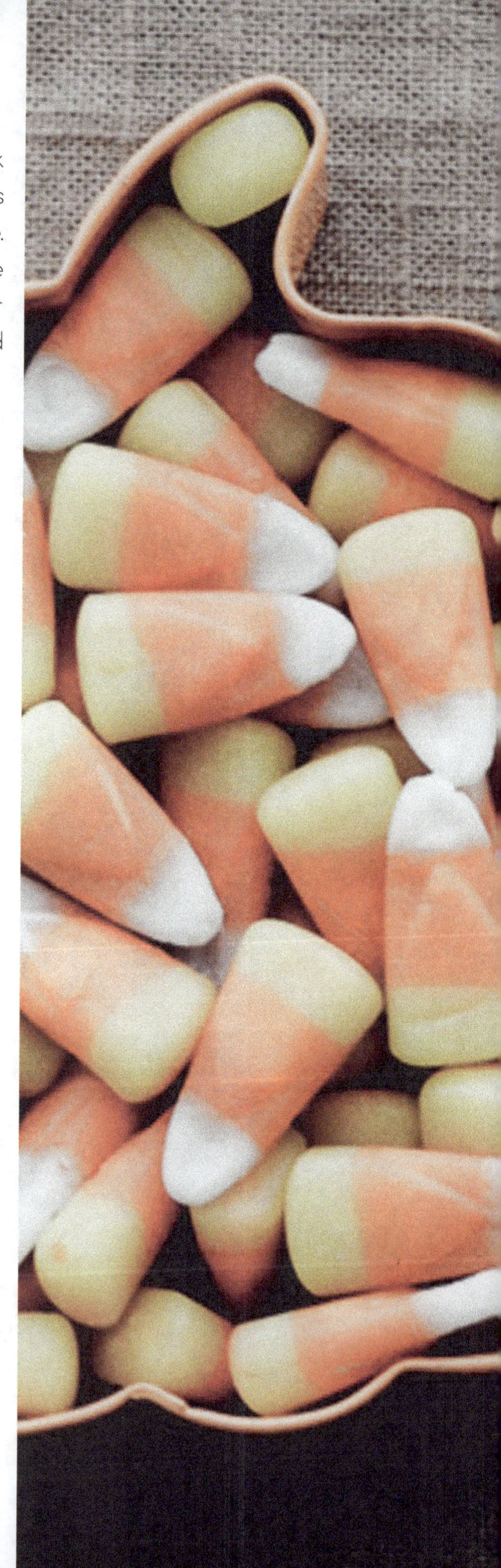

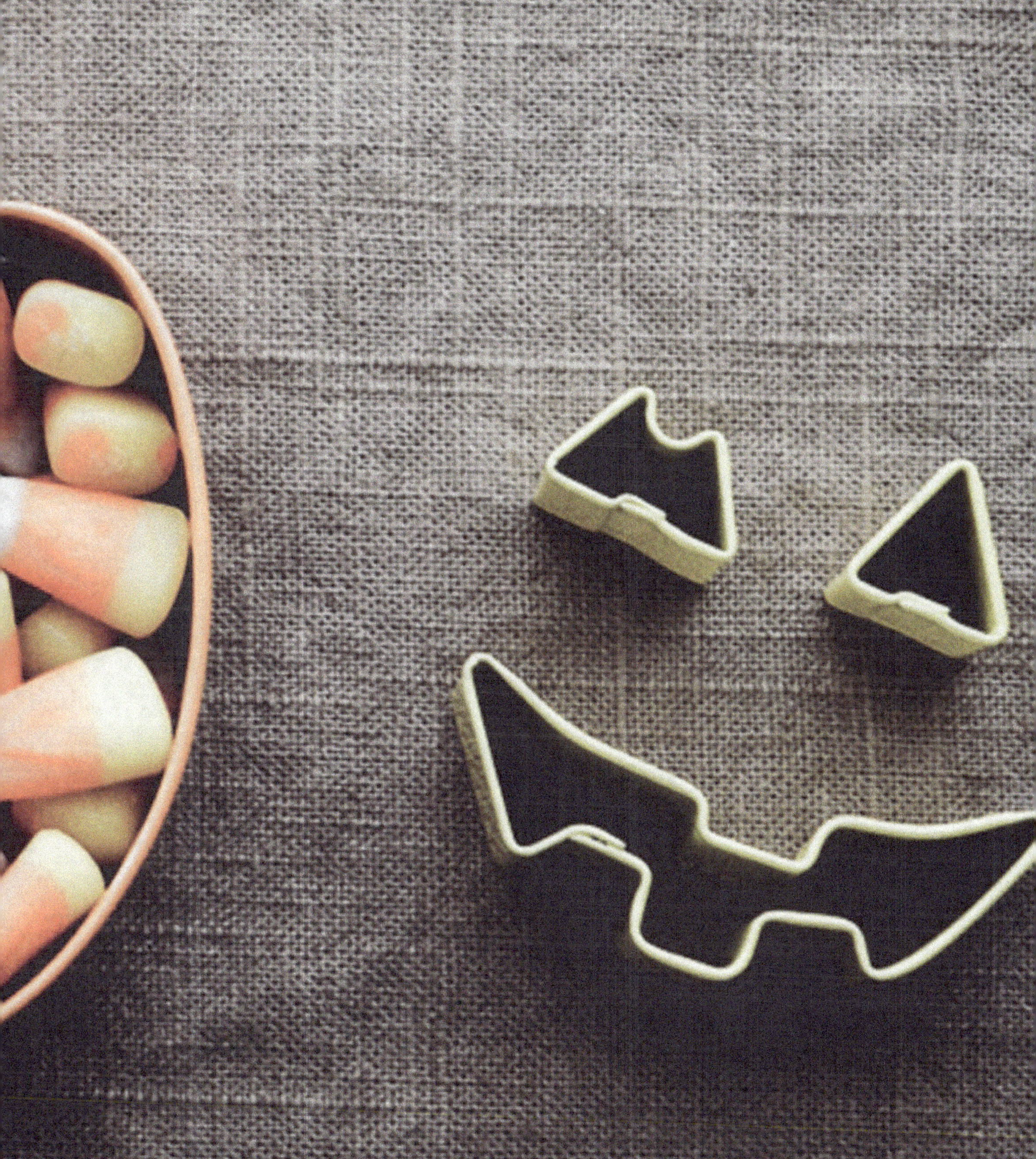

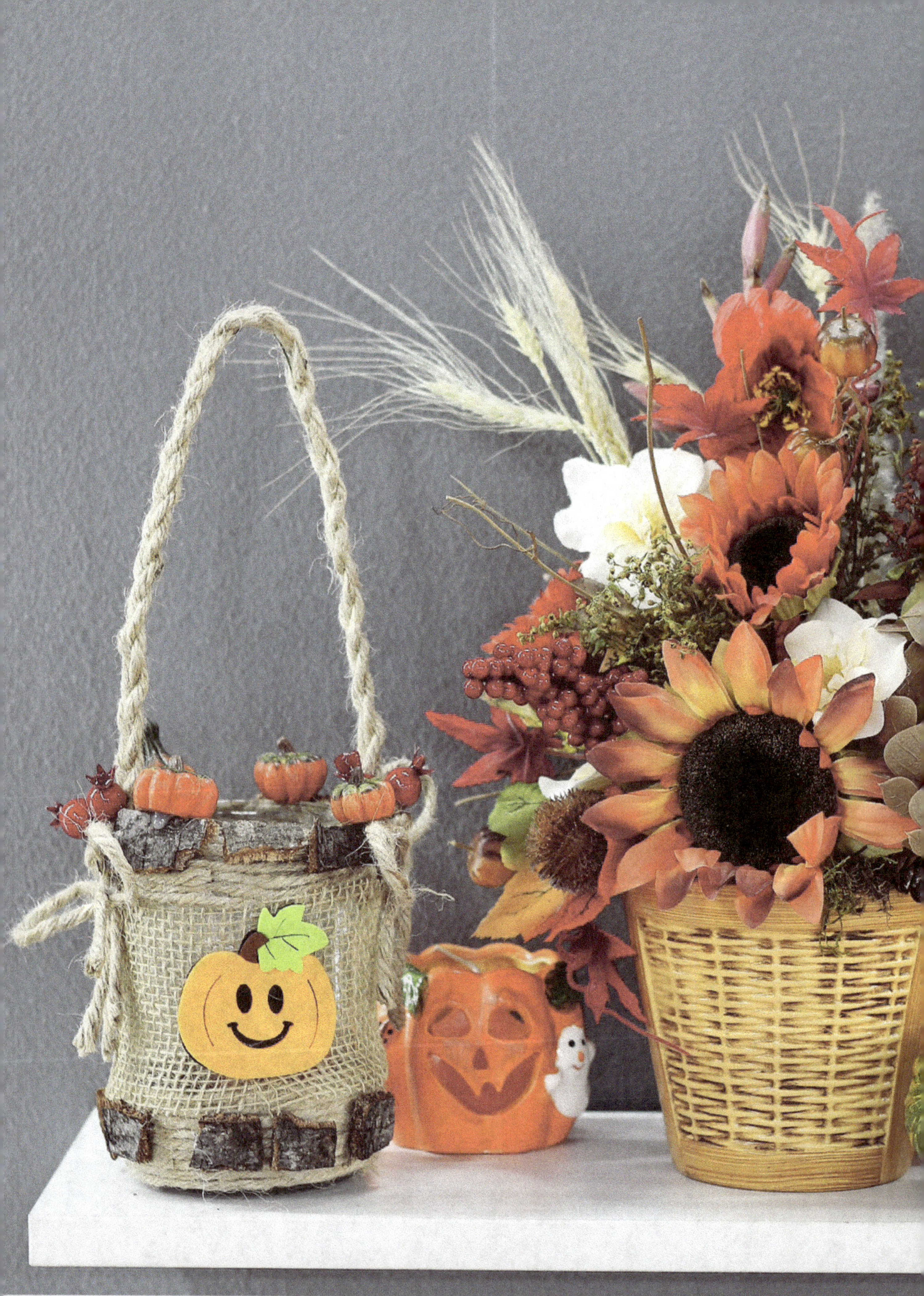

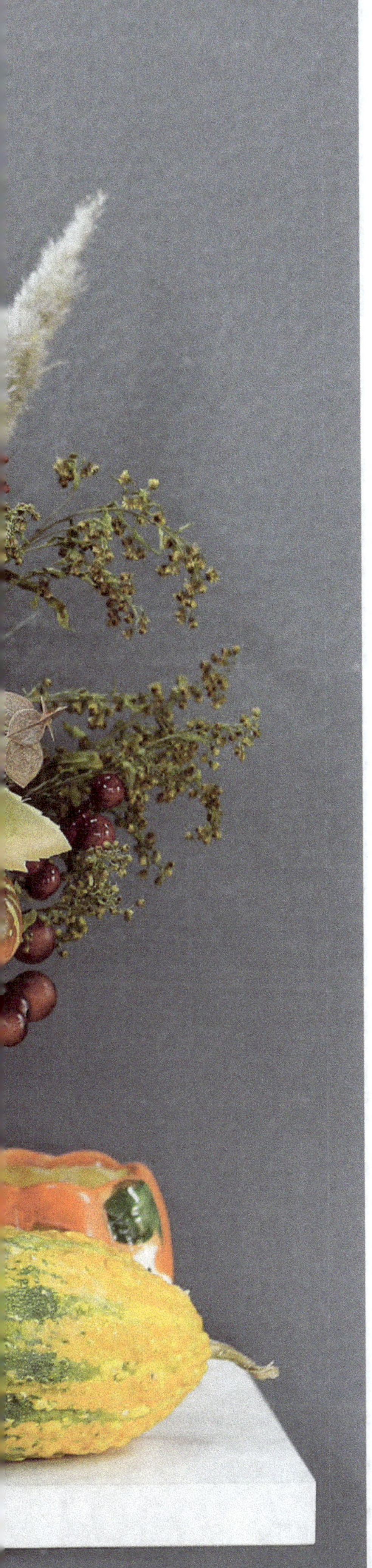

which can be edited individually. You can edit either or both the image as needed. For example, you could resize the image based on your craft bag's size and change the color or fill in a pattern in the image by selecting the image, clicking on the appropriate tool on the "Edit Bar," as shown in the picture below. Click on "Group" to have a composite design and then copy-paste for the number of times you want to print the design.

Click on "Save" at the top right corner of the screen and give the desired name to the project, for example, "trick or treat bag," and click "Save."

Now, your design is ready to be printed. Simply click on the "Make It" button on the top right corner of the screen. You will see the required mats and material displayed on the screen.

Click "Continue" at the bottom right corner of the screen after you have loaded the vinyl to the "Cricut" machine and print the design onto the paper.

Note - The image used is available for purchase, so click on "Purchase" at the bottom right of the screen to buy the pictures before you can print them. And once you have made the purchase, the "Continue" button will be available to you.

Calibrate the machine with your device and use the appropriate setting to cut your chosen material. Place the vinyl on top of the cutting mat and load it into the "Cricut" machine by pushing against the rollers. The "Load/Unload" button will start flashing, so just press it. Then

press the "Go" button, which would already be flashing.

Carefully remove the excess vinyl from the sheet.
To easily paste your design on the craft bag without stretching the pieces, put the transfer tape on
top of the cut design. Now, slowly peel the paper
backing on the vinyl from one end to the other
in a rolling motion to ensure even placement and
use the scraper tool on top of the transfer tape
to remove any bubbles, and then just peel off the
transfer tape. Viola! You have your own customized
Halloween trick or treat bags that may look like the
picture below.

TREAT BAG TOPPER

SUPPLIES NEEDED

- "Cricut Maker"
- standard grip mat
- scoring wheel
- adhesive for paper
- hot glue gun
- cardstock in desired colors (green,
  yellow, white)

INSTRUCTIONS:

Login to "Design Space" using your "Cricut" ID and
click on "New Project" to view a blank Canvas
Let's use an already existing project from the
"Cricut" library and customize it. So, click on the
"Projects" icon on the "Design Panel" and click on

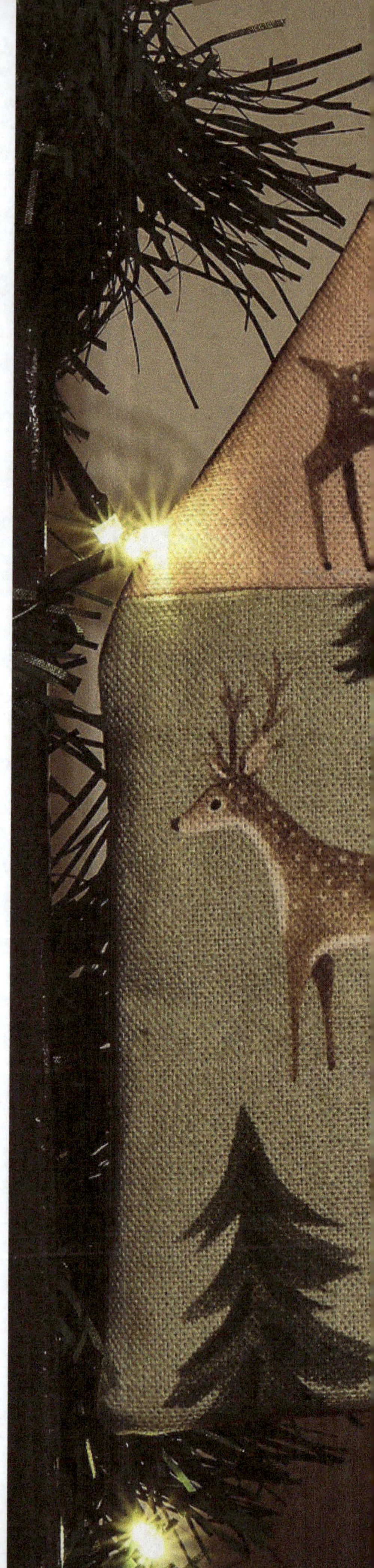

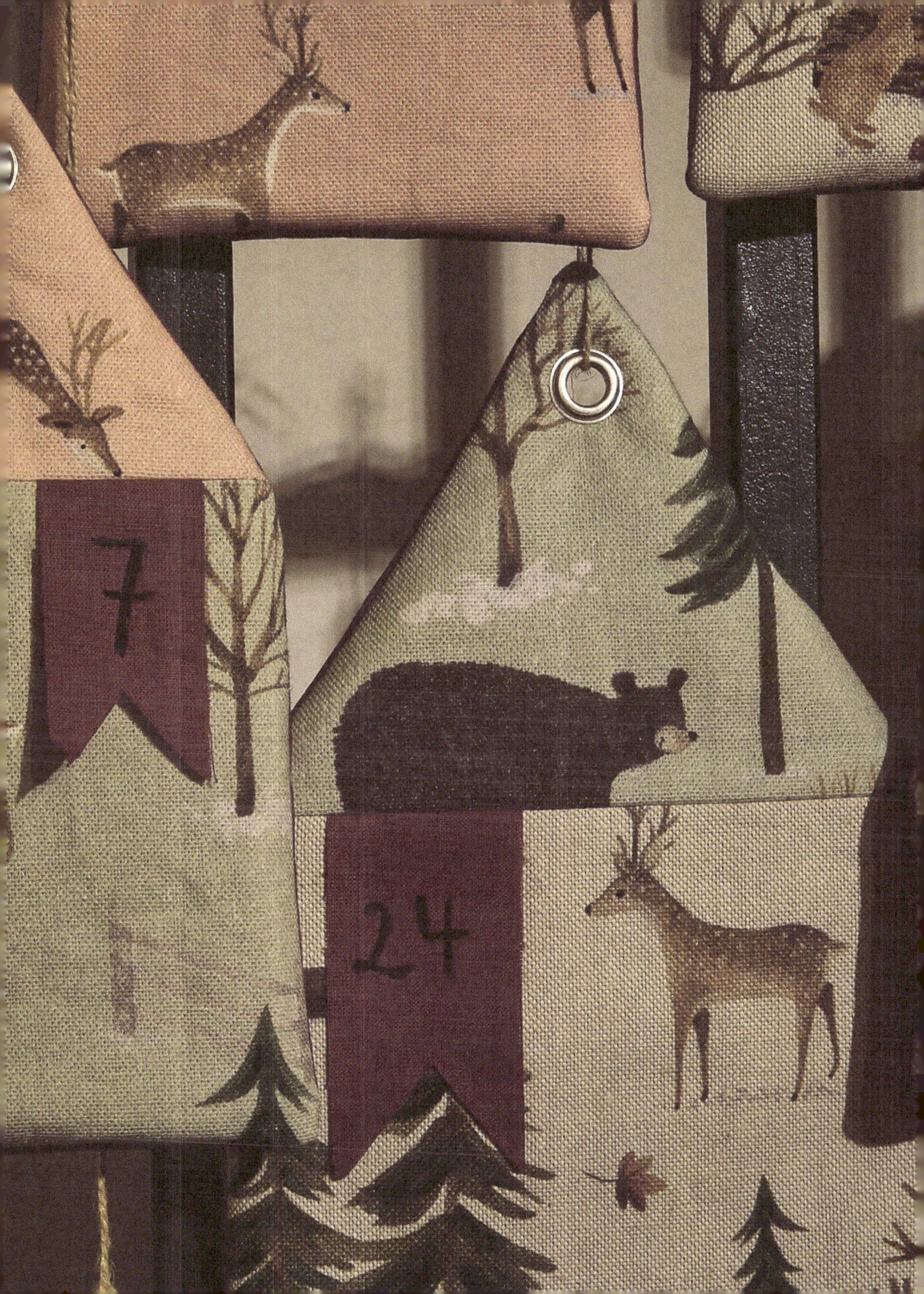

7
24

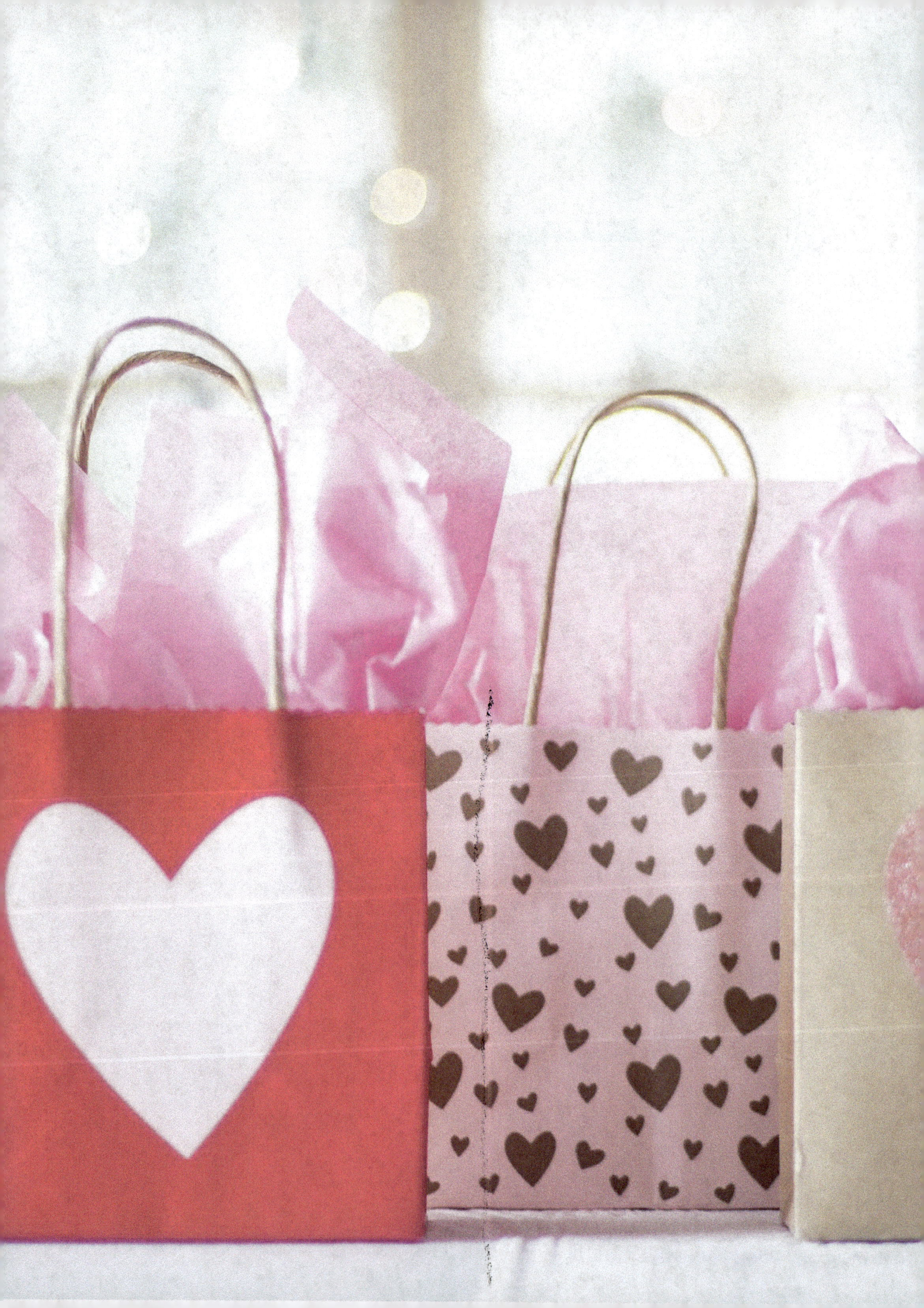

the "All Categories" drop-down menu to view all existing projects that you can select from. For this example, we will click on "Parties & Events" then type in "bag topper" in the search bar to narrow down your search.

You can view all the projects available by clicking on them, and a pop-up window displaying all the details of the project will appear on your screen. The project selected for this example is shown in the picture below.

Click on "Customize" so you can edit the project to your preference.

The selected design will be displayed on the Canvas. In the "Layers Panel," you can see that this design has multiple layers that can be edited individually but let's not mess with the scoring and rearrangement. If you would like to change the design color, select the cut layer and click on the "Linetype Swatch" to view the color palette and choose the desired color, as shown in the picture below.

(Note - There are other images and layers displayed on the "Layers Panel" for this project that you can ignore).

Now, your design is ready to be cut and scored. Simply click on the "Make It" button on the top right corner of the screen. You will see the required mats and material displayed on the screen. Set the material to "Cardstock."

Click "Continue" at the bottom right corner of the screen after loading the cardstock to the "Cricut" machine.

Note - The image used is available for purchase, so click on "Purchase" at the bottom right of the screen to buy the photos before you can print them. And once you have made the purchase, the "Continue" button will be available to you.

Once the machine has completed cutting the design, it will stop, and you will be prompted by "Design Space" to mount the scoring wheel in "clamp B" of the adaptive tool system.

Now you are ready to fold the cardstock along the scored lines and assemble the topper using adhesive on the yellow and green cardstock to top them up with the white cardstock. After the topper has been made, use the hot glue gun to close the bag topper over your craft bag or cello bag filled with treats.

CAKE TOPPER

SUPPLIES NEEDED

- "Cricut Maker"
- standard grip mat
- hot glue gun
- bamboo skewer or wooden dowel
- cardstock in desired colors (green, yellow, white)

INSTRUCTIONS:

Login to "Design Space" using your "Cricut" ID and click on "New Project" to view a blank Canvas
Let's use text for this project. Click on "Text" from the "Designs Panel" on the left of the screen and type in "It's a…" then press enter and type "GIRL" (add spaces before this to bring the "GIRL" right under the last "." of the preceding text, as shown

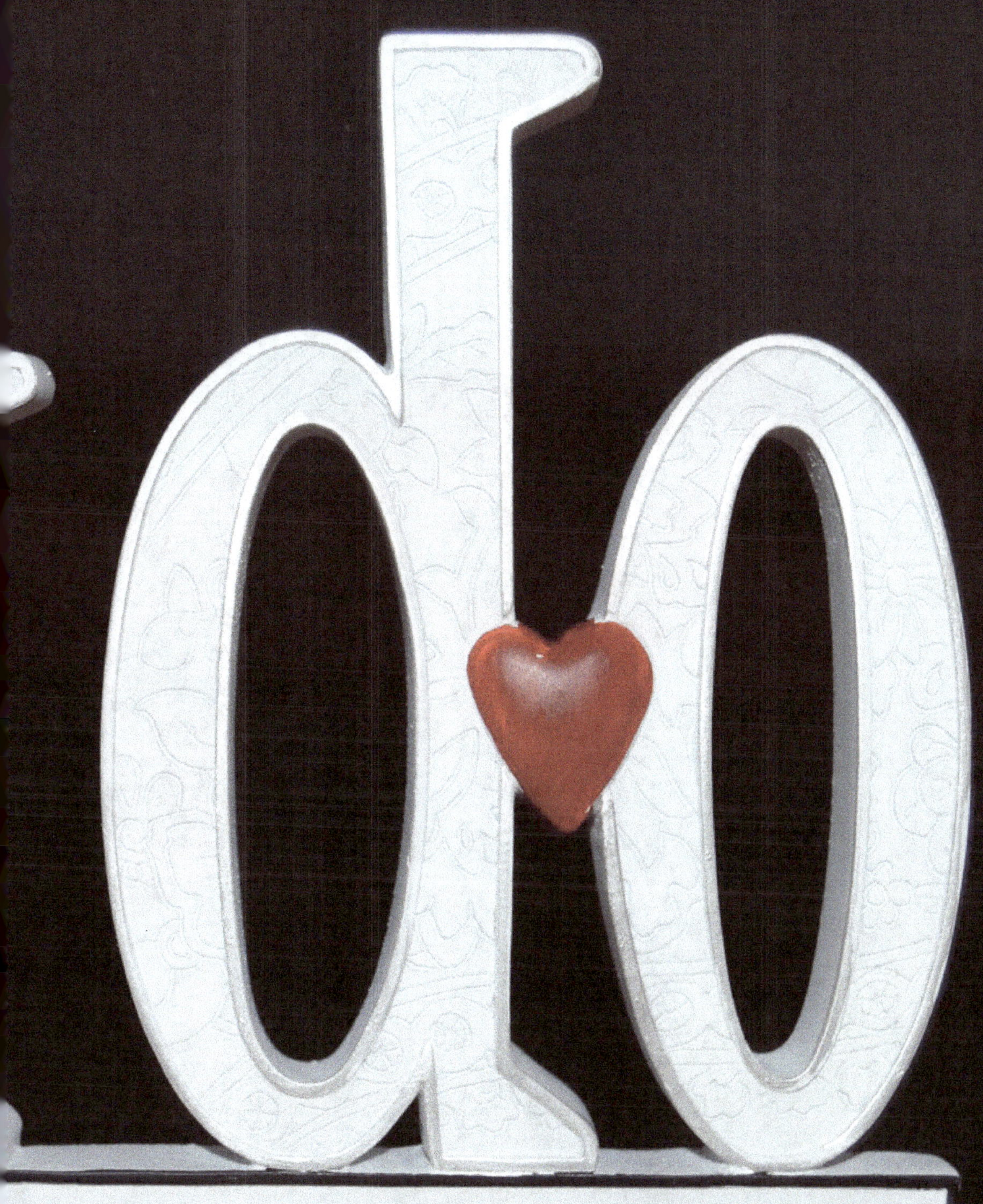
do
DAY AND ALWAYS

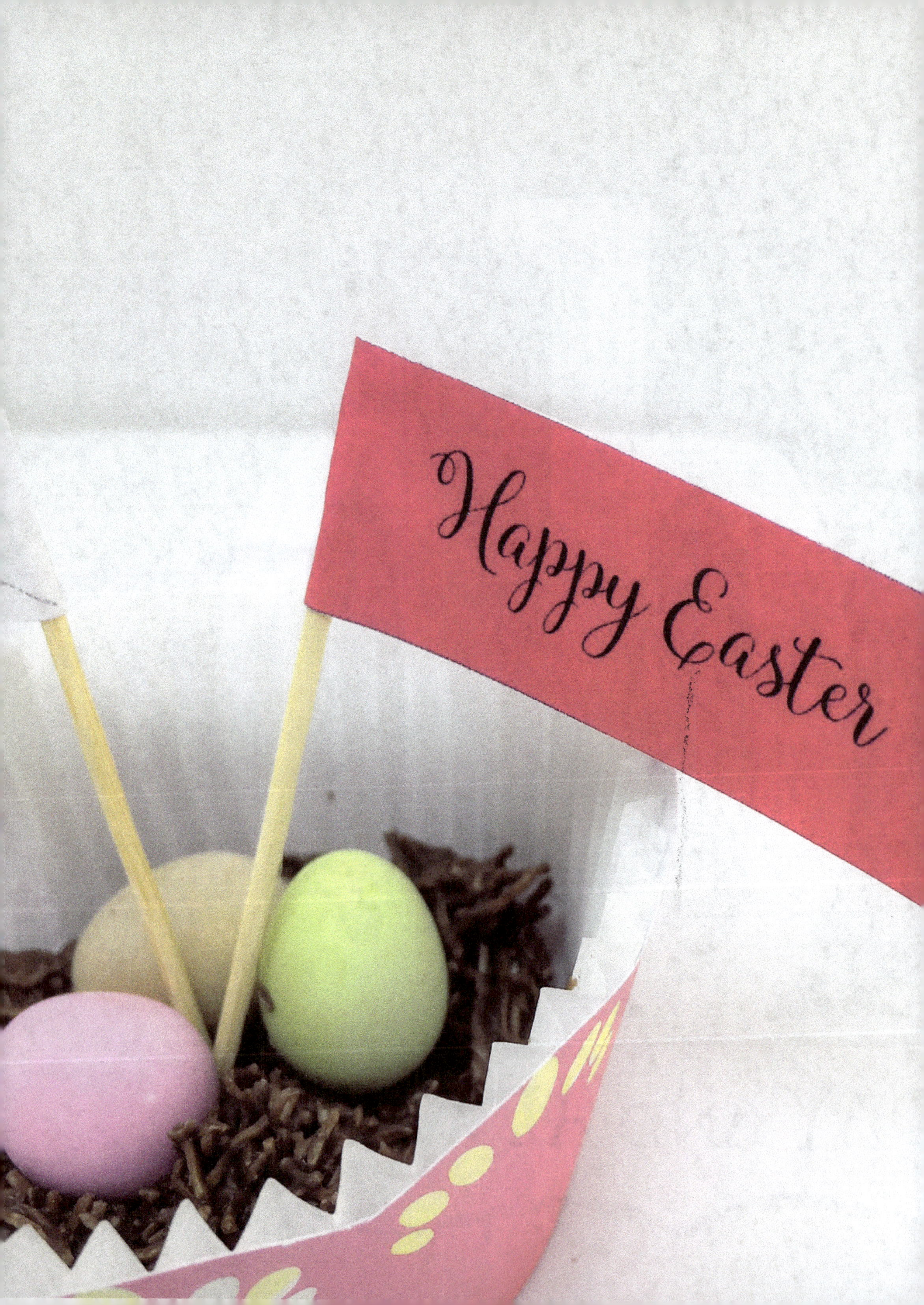

Happy Easter

in the picture below.

Click on "Alignment" then "Center" to align the text as shown in the picture below (you may need to adjust the spacing here depending on how big you want your cake topper to be). The font "3 Birds On Paradise" in Regular and color, as shown in the picture below, were selected for the image below. But you can let your creativity take over this step and choose any color or font you like.

Click on "Save" at the top right corner of the screen and give the desired name to the project, for example, "Cake Topper - It's a Girl," and click "Save." Simply click on the "Make It" button on the top right corner of the screen. You will see the required mats and material displayed on the screen.

Note - The font used is available for purchase, so click on "Purchase" at the bottom right of the screen to buy the images before you can print them. And once you have made the purchase, the "Continue" button will be available to you.

Calibrate the machine with your device and use the appropriate setting to cut your chosen material. Place the cardstock on top of the cutting mat and load it into the "Cricut" machine by pushing against the rollers. The "Load/Unload" button will start flashing, so just press it. Then press the "Go" button, which would already be flashing.

Now use the hot glue gun to adhere the design onto a bamboo skewer or wooden dowel, and Viola! You have your customized cake topper that may look like the picture below.

FELT ROSES

SUPPLIES NEEDED

- SVG files with 3D flower design
- Felt Sheets
- Fabric Grip Mat
- Glue Gun

INSTRUCTIONS:

First of all, upload your Flower SVG Graphics into the Cricut design space. ("How to import images into Cricut Design Space)

Having placed the image in the project, select it, right-click and click "Ungroup." This allows you to resize each flower independently of the others. Since you are using felt, it is recommended that each of the flowers is at least 6 inches in size.

Create several copies of the flowers, as many as you wish, selecting the colors you want in the Color Sync Panel (by dragging and dropping the images into the color you would like them to be cut on). Immediately you're through with that, click on "Make it" on the Cricut design space.

Click on "Continue." After your Cricut Maker is connected and registered, under the 'materials' options, select "Felt."

If your rotary blade is not in the machine, insert it. Place the first felt sheet on the Fabric Grip Mat (in order of color), then load them into your Cricut Maker. Press the "cut" button when this is done.

After they are cut, begin to roll the cut flowers one

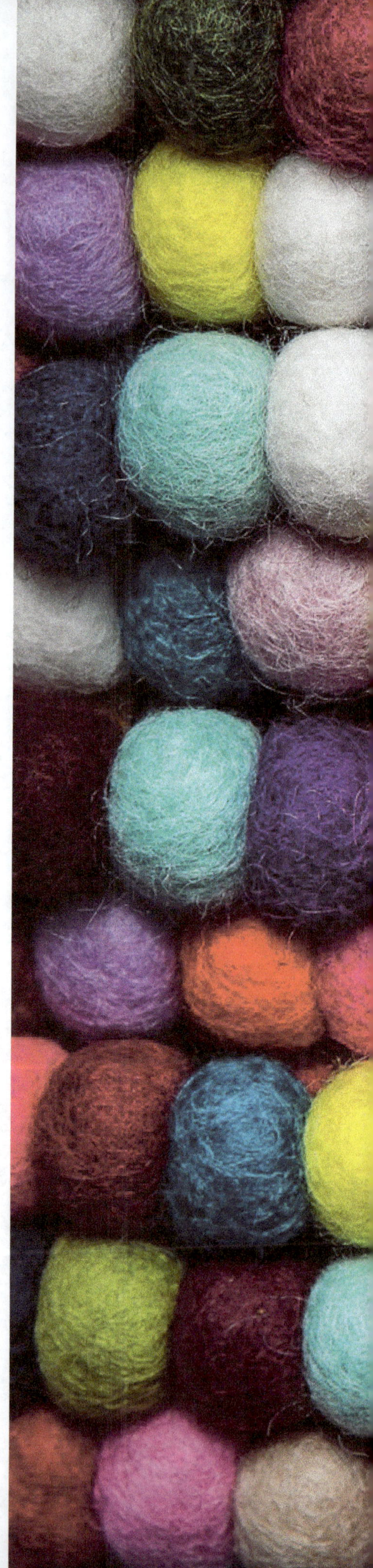

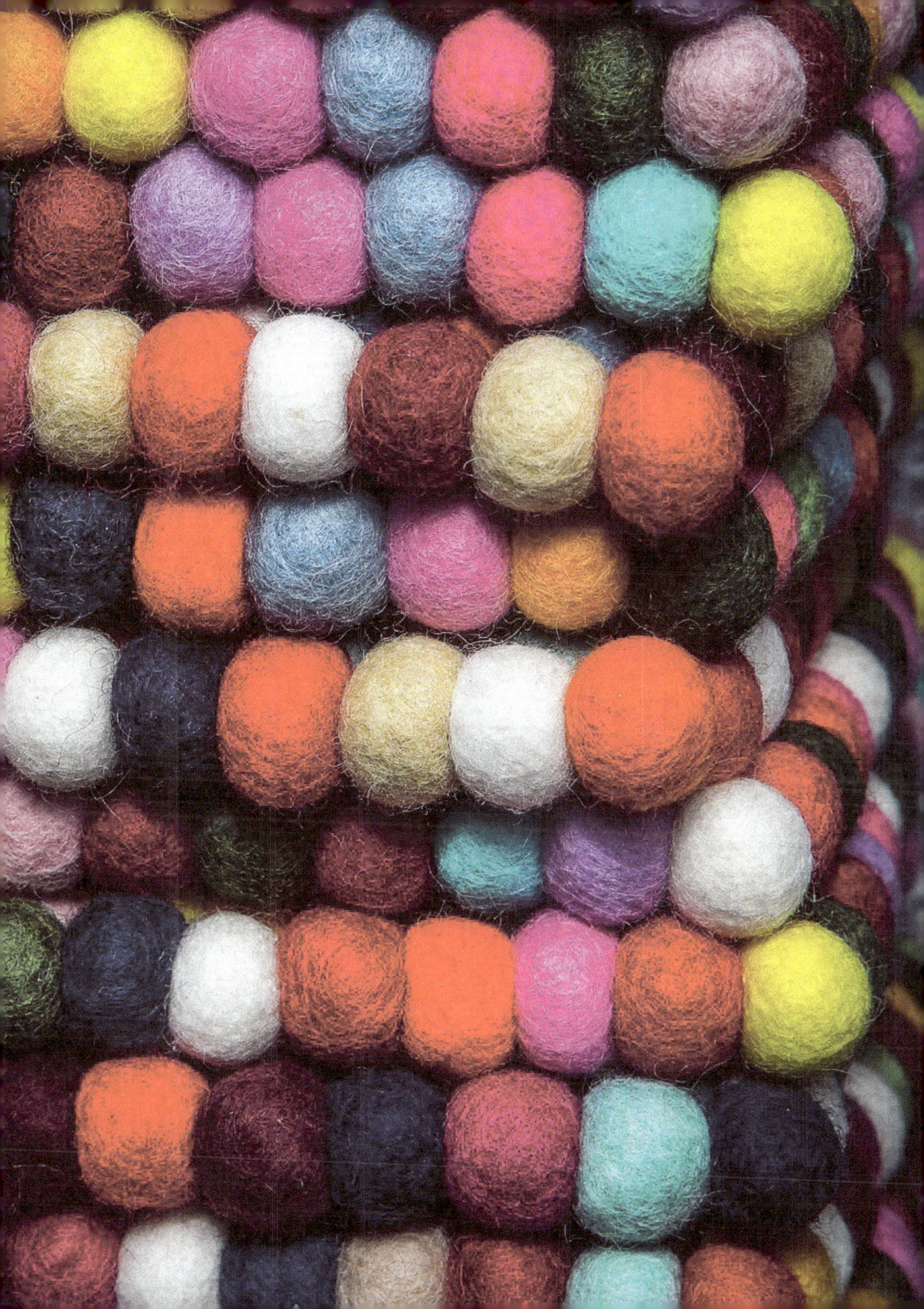

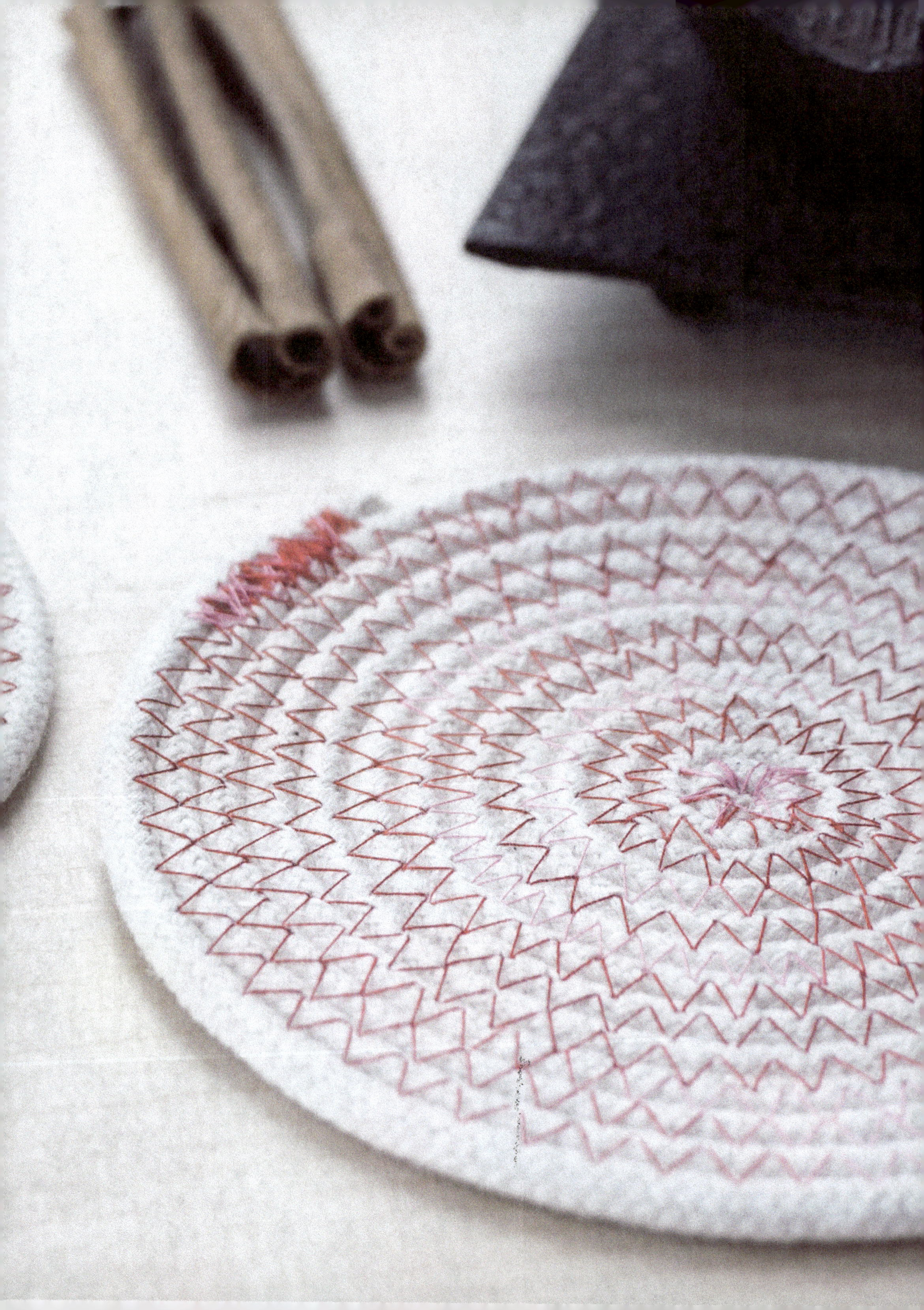

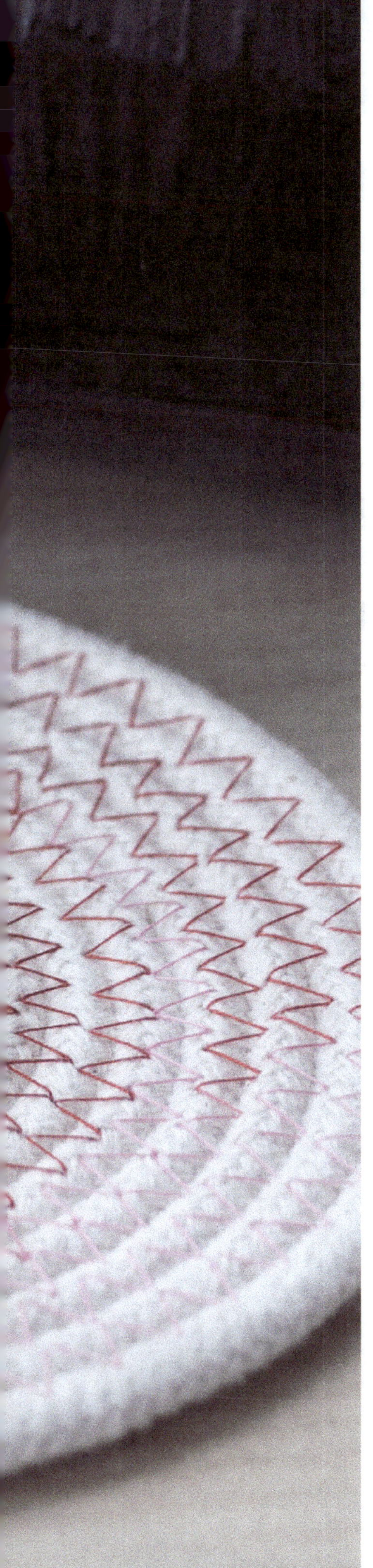

by one. Do this from the outside in. Make sure that you do not move them too tight. Use the picture as a guide.

Apply Hot Glue on the circle right in the middle and press the felt flowers you rolled up on the glue. Hold this in place, and do not let it go until the bond binds it.

Wait for the glue to dry, and your roses are ready for use.

CUSTOM COASTERS

SUPPLIES NEEDED

- Free Pattern Templates
- Monogram Design (in Design Space)
- Cardstock or Printing Paper
- Butcher Paper
- Lint-free towel
- Round Coaster Blanks
- LightGrip Mat
- EasyPress 2 (6" x 7" recommended)
- EasyPress Mat
- Infusible Ink Pens
- Heat Resistant Tape
- Cricut BrightPad (optional) for easier tracing)

INSTRUCTIONS:

1. In Cricut Design Space, open the monogram design. You can click "Customize" and choose the techniques that you want to cut out, or just go ahead and cut out all the letters.

2. Click on "Make It."

3. On the page displayed, click on "Mirror Image"
   to make the image mirrored. This must be done
   whenever you are using infusible ink. For your
   material, choose "Cardstock." Then, place your
   cardstock on the mat, load it into the machine,
   then press the "Cut" button on the Cricut
   machine.

4. After the Cricut machine is done cutting, unload it
   and remove the done monograms from the
   mat.

5. Trace the designs onto the cut-out. If you have
   a Cricut BrightPad, you can use it to carry out
   this step much more efficiently, as it will make
   the trace lines easier to identify. Tracing should
   be done using Cricut Infusible Ink Pens.

6. Use the lint-free towel to wipe the coaster. Ensure
   that no residue is left behind to prevent any
   marks from being left on the blank.

7. Make the design centered on the face down
   coaster.

8. Get a piece of butcher paper that is an inch
   larger on each side of the coaster, place it on
   top of the design.

9. Tape this butcher paper onto the coaster using
   heat-resistant tape to hold the design fast.

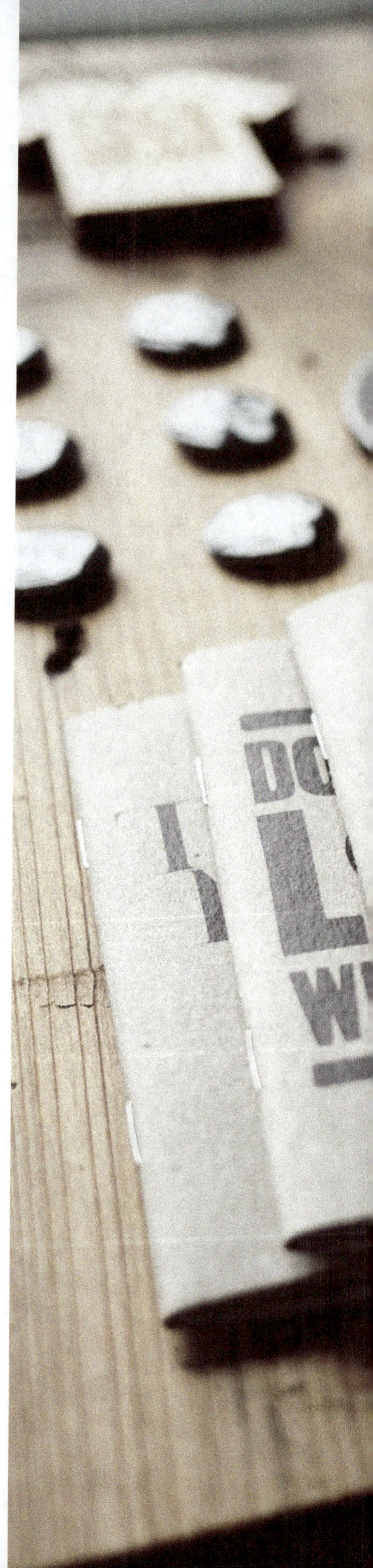

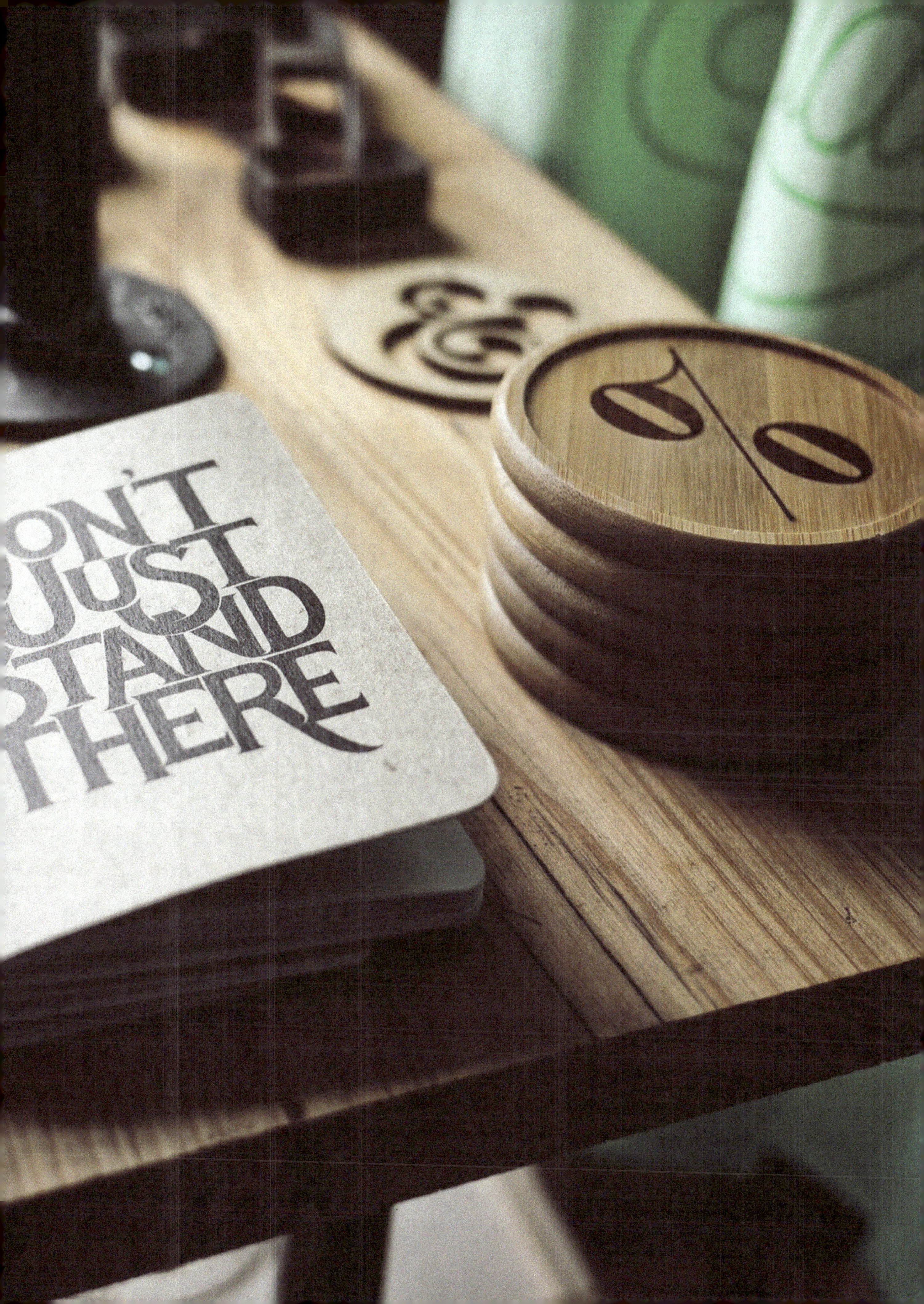
DON'T
JUST
STAND
THERE

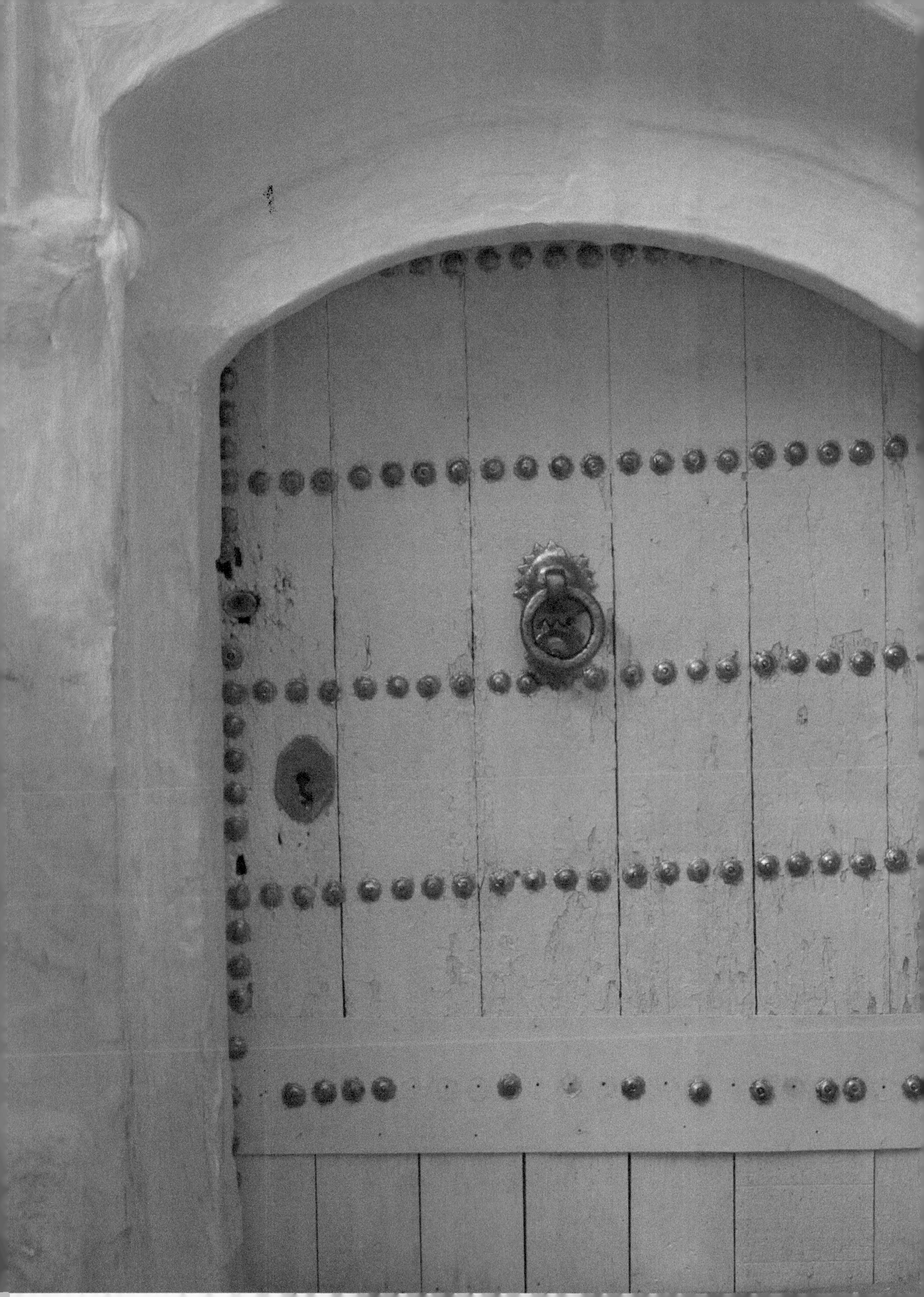

10. Set the temperature of your EasyPress to 400 degrees and set the timer to 240 seconds.

11. Place another butcher paper piece on your EasyPress mat, set the coaster on top of it, face up.

12. Place another piece of butcher paper on top. Place the already preheated EasyPress on top of the coaster and start the timer.

13. Lightly hold the EasyPress in place (without mo ving) or leave it in place right on the coaster - if on a perfectly flat surface - till the timer goes off.

14. After this is done, gently remove the EasyPress 2, then turn it off.

15. The coaster will be very hot, so you should leave it to get calm before touching it. When it is cool, you can peel the design off of it.

CUSTOMIZED DOORMAT

SUPPLIES NEEDED

- Cricut Machine
- Scrap cardstock (The color does not matter)
- Coir mat (18" x 30")
- Outdoor acrylic paint
- Vinyl stencil

- Transfer tape
- Flat round paintbrush
- Cutting mat (12" x 24")

INSTRUCTIONS:

1. Create your design in Cricut Design Space. You can also download an SVG format of your choice and import it into Cricut Design Space. Make sure that your plan is the right size; resize it to ensure that this is so.

2. Next, you are to cut the stencil. You do this by clicking "Make it" in Cricut Design Space when done with the design. After this, you select "Card stock" as the material. Then, you press the "Cut" button on the Cricut machine.

3. When this is done, remove the stencil from the machine and weed.

4. Next, on the reverse side of the stencil, apply spray glue. After this, attach the stencil to the doormat, exactly where you want your design to be; then, pick up the letter bits left on the cutting mat and glue them to their places in the stencil on the doormat.

5. The next step is to mask the doormat's parts that you do not want to paint on. You can do this using painters' plastic.

6. Now, it's time to spray-paint your stencil on the doormat. Keeping the paint can about 5 inches away from the doormat, spray up and down,

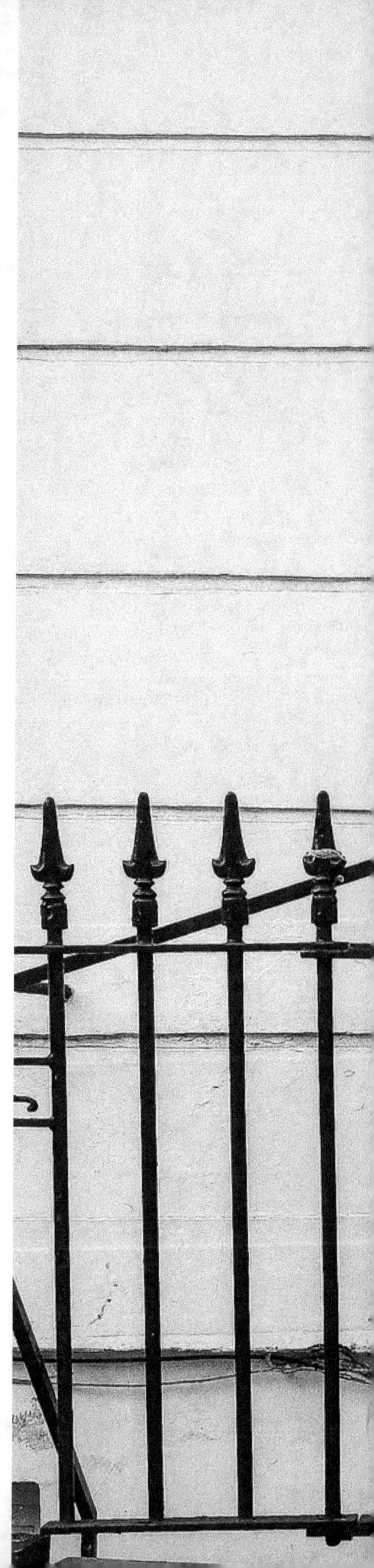

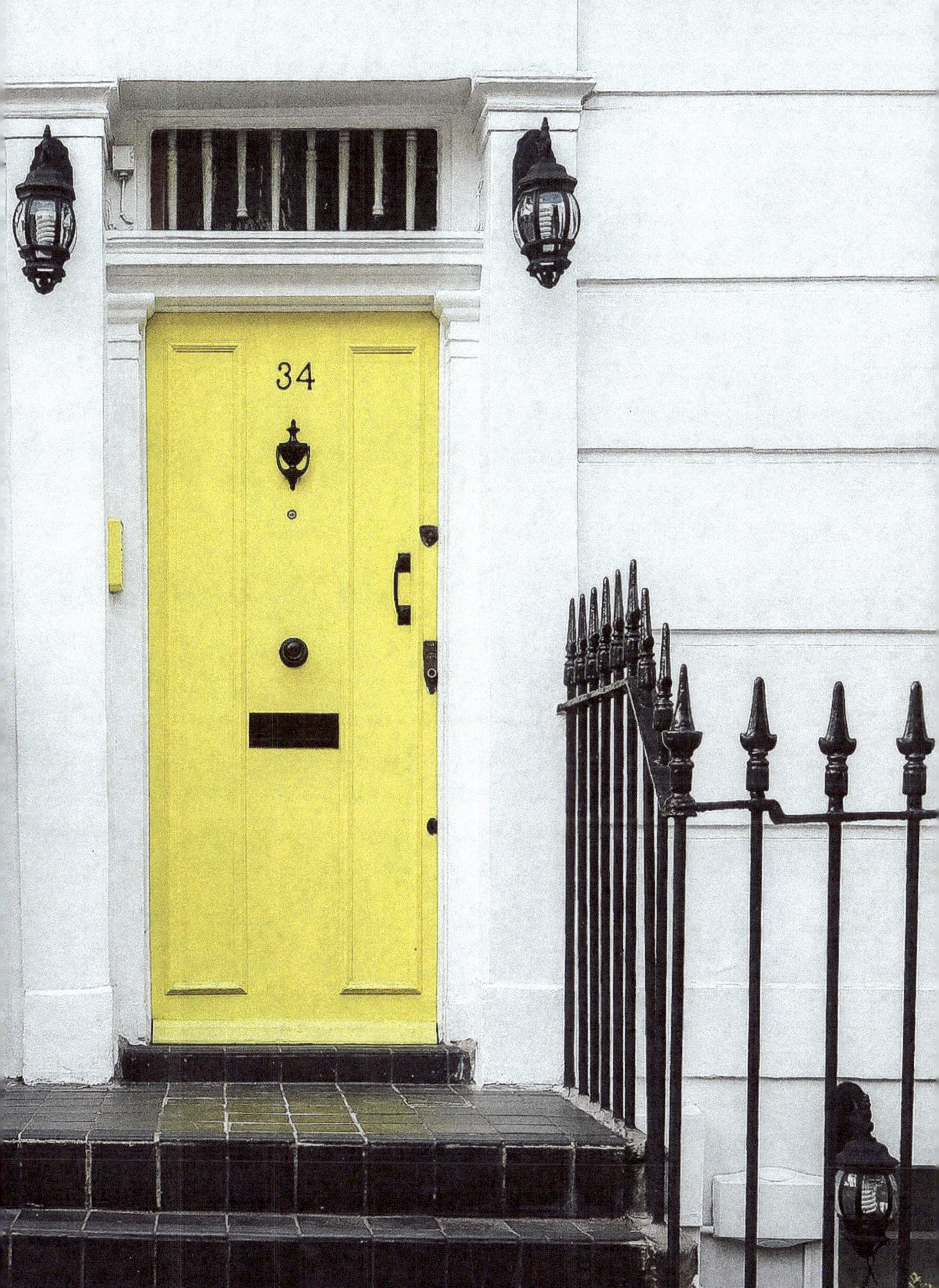

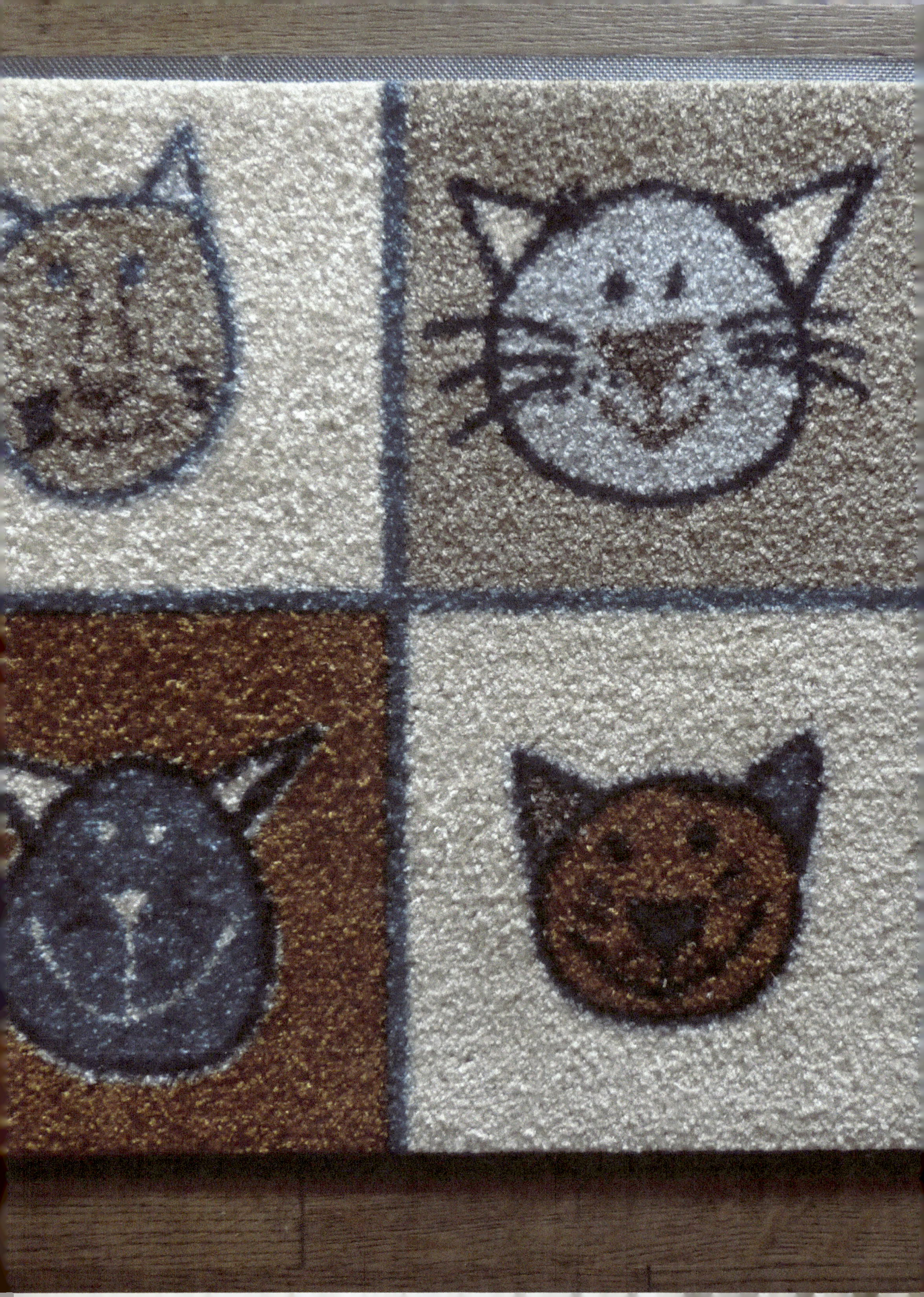

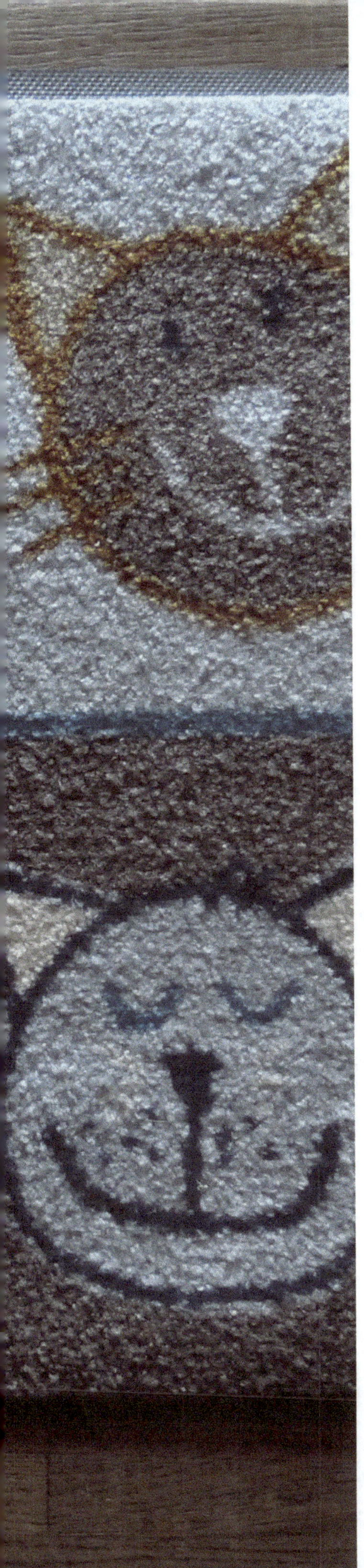

keeping the can point straight through the stencil. If it is at an angle, the paint will get under the stencil and ruin your design. Spray the entire stencil 2-3 times to ensure that you do not miss any part and that the paint is even.

7.   You're just about done! Now, remove the masking plastic and the stencil and leave the doormat for about one hour to get dry.

Chapter 4
The Business Side of Things and Ideas to Earn

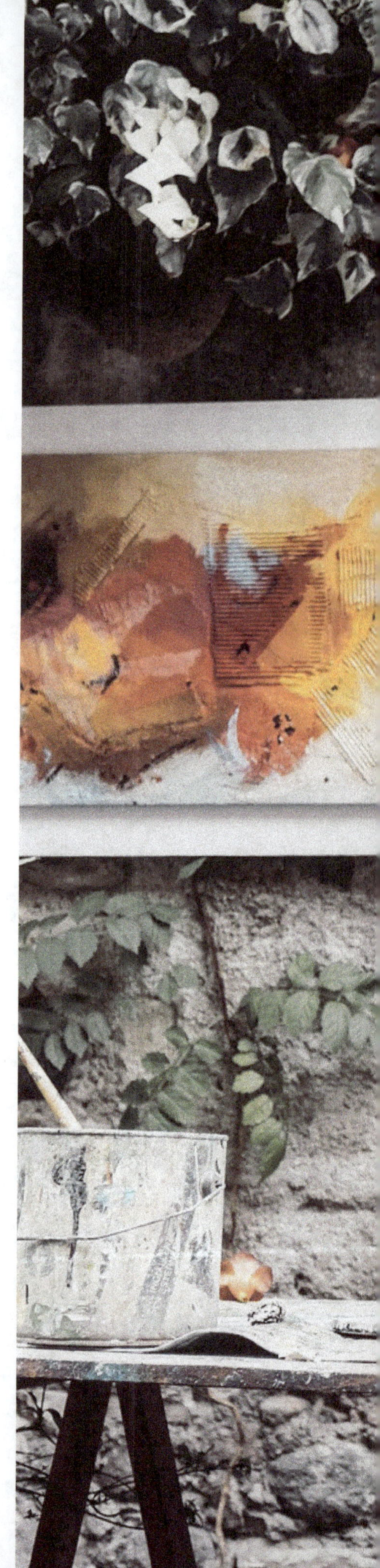

Your designs' creativity and the skill you will develop can allow you to create and start your own business if you wish. For enthusiastic novices, many questions would be faced, such as:

1) WHERE DO I START?

Like any start-up business, initial questions need to be addressed to overcome possible difficulties. For example, addressing issues like defining my clientele, the products that might be of interest, where to find them, and how to make a profit margin of my sales are essential to tackle from the start. In other words, you will need a useful and well-defined business strategy to start with.

2) CHOOSING MY CLIENT

You can target two avenues to sell your products: either by looking at how you can approach the market locally or online. It is advisable to concentrate efforts on one approach to start with as your target is to generate profits as soon as possible. Never forget that your goal is to grow, benefit and reinvest it so that your business expands. The quicker you

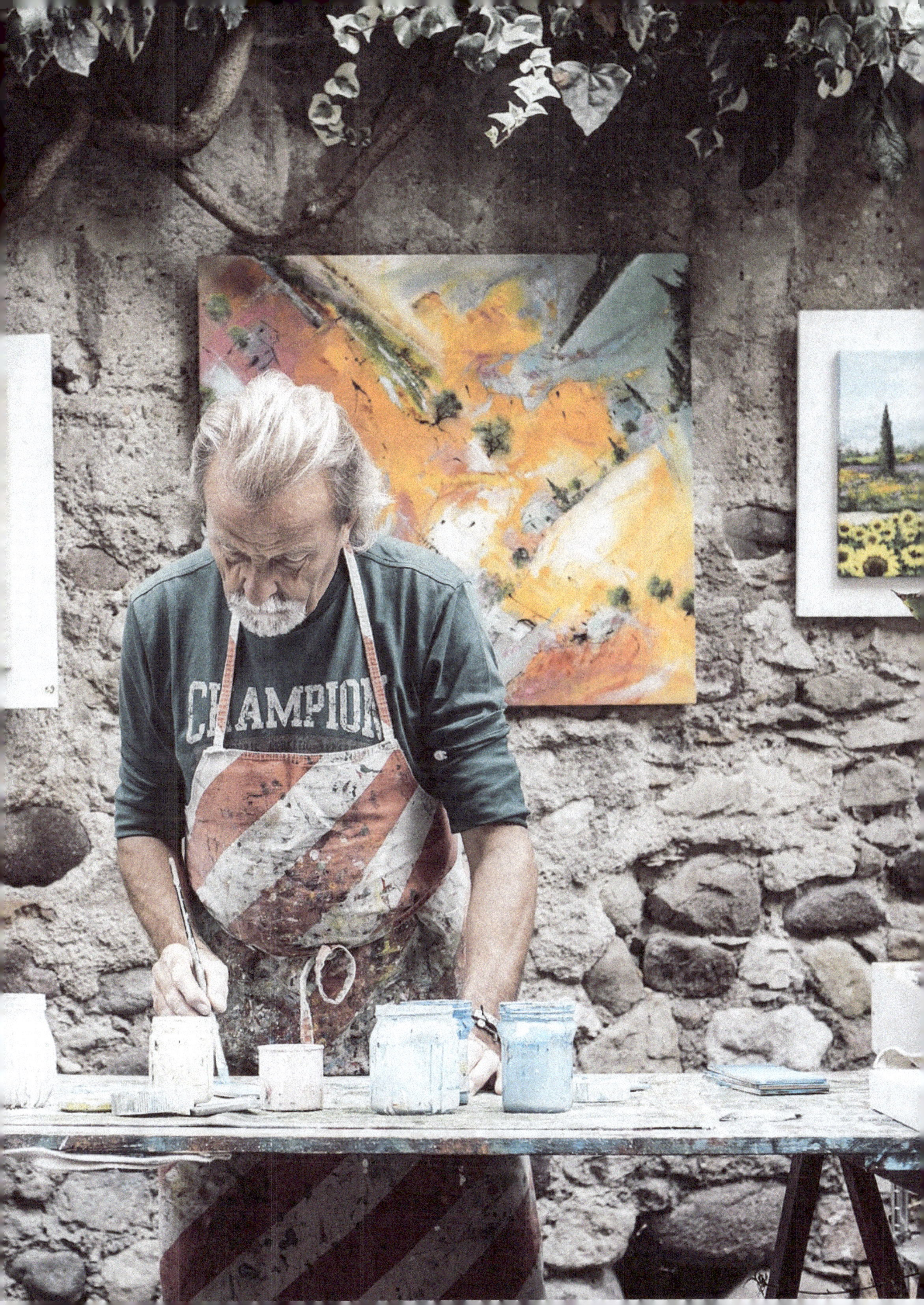

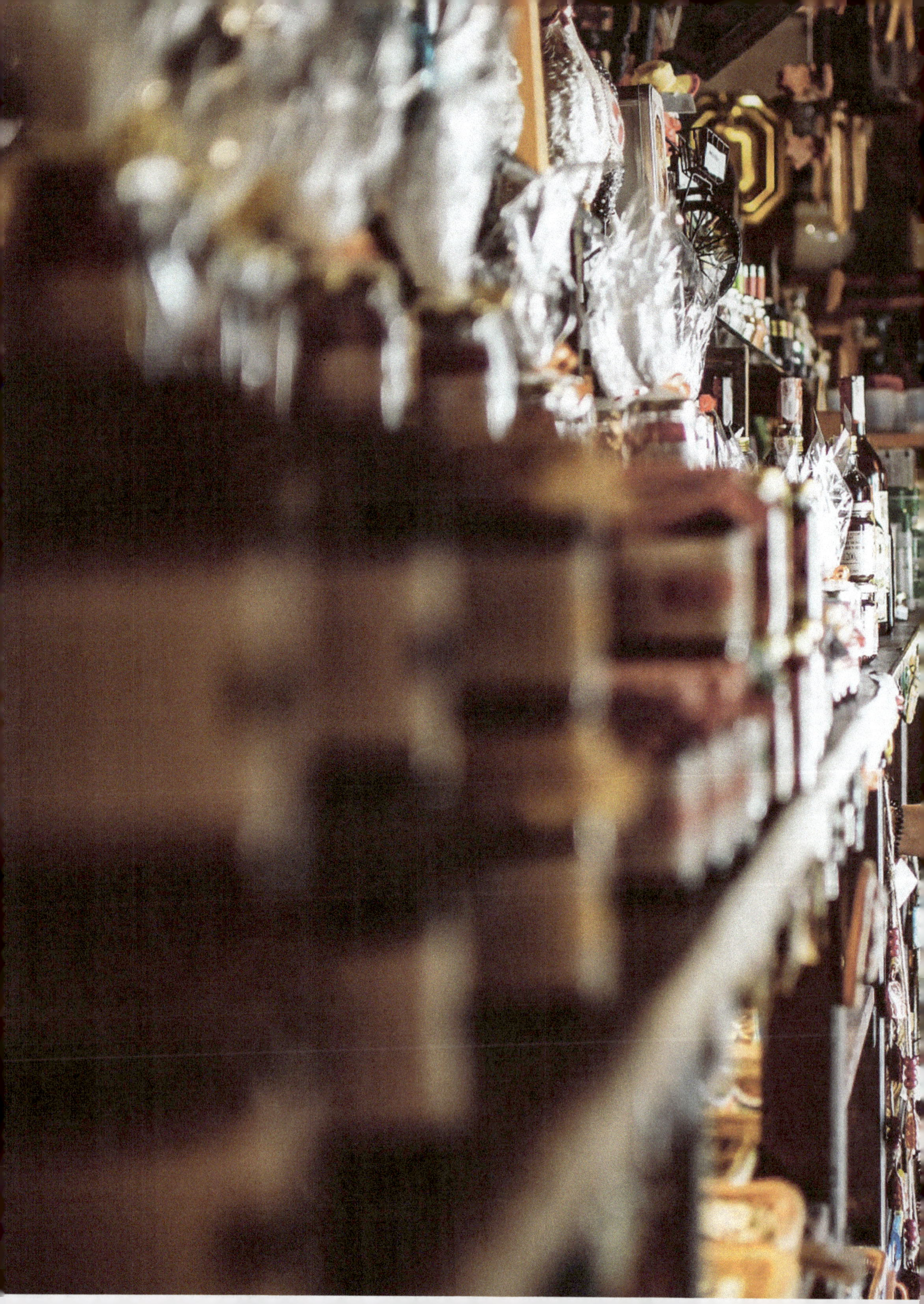

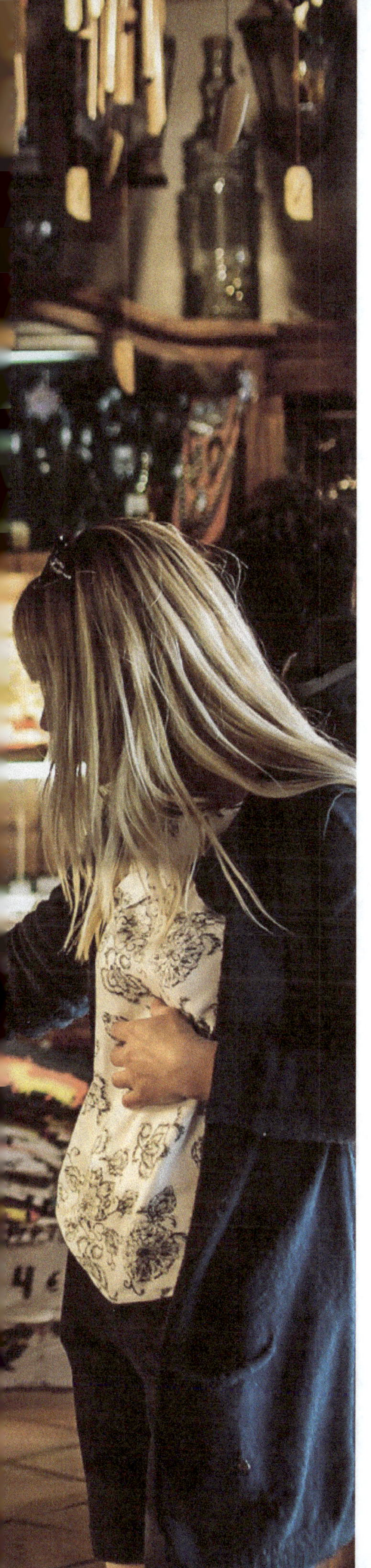

increase your sales, the more likely you will reinvest in new tools or new products, making, in turn, a more substantial financial turnover. Understanding your marketing strategy is key to your success.

21) APPROACHING LOCAL MARKETS

You can explore selling your products from 'business to business. In this configuration, the volume of sales is important as the larger the production, the lower the production cost per item is. This is the most challenging balance to reach for a new Cricut-based business. The advantage of obtaining contractual work means you can negotiate to buy a large quantity from vendors. However, such 'golden' opportunities are hard to find since such contracts are opened to competition. Yet, as a new start-up business, you can present your products specifically tailored for business customers. A custom work approach offers positive aspects as firms always look for originality and useful products. By creating such a relationship, your business is likely to become a point of reference for future other contacts, hence launching many upselling opportunities. However, it is essential to bear in mind that finding such a niche is hard as competition is very stiff!

Another approach to consider for selling your products is from 'business to customer.' In this model, though the sales volume remains important, your objective is to present your products to retail customers willing to buy them. Creativity, imagination will be keys to your success, as well as what type of media and medium you want to work in (e.g., T-shirts, mugs). Equally important is a retail space you will need to choose to offer your items. Experiencing different locations and products is all part of the efforts of a new start-up business. Also, a custom work approach for local customers will present advantages since the startup costs are the lowest of all the different strategies described. However, as a new business in the field, starting can be difficult. Word of mouth can be your first step, and produce the right products at an affordable price.

22) SELLING ONLINE

If you are adept at higher technical knowledge, you can generate significant benefits by providing quality custom work, bulk offering, or information network. It is advisable to concentrate your efforts on one approach to start with. If you choose, for example, a custom work approach, you increase the chances to find potential customers looking for your products as they turn to a search engine like Google to see what they are looking for. Websites like Amazon Handmade or Etsy provide an excellent platform to allow selling custom design services. Equally efficient is the launch of your site. This strategy is worth looking at. Selling online presents advantages such as low startup costs and access to the global market with access to millions of potential customers.
Furthermore, online custom prices tend to be lower than those on the local market. However, access to the global market means that competition is stiff, pushing products competitively. Selling online requires specific knowledge in logistics as far as shipping and packing your products are concerned, a cost factor that needs to be considered in your pricing.
eBay and Amazon have become the largest platforms. On the other hand, if an online retail business

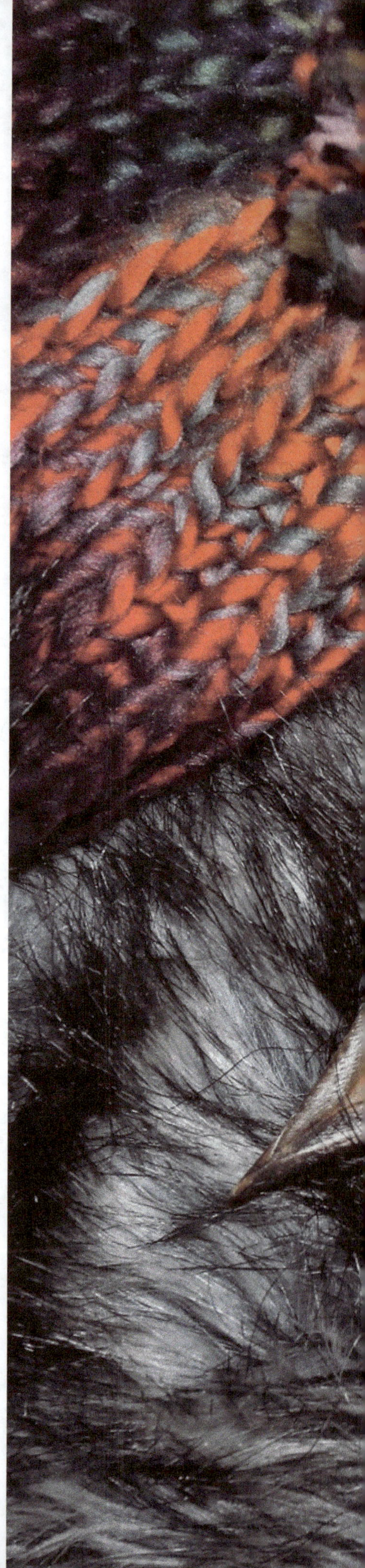

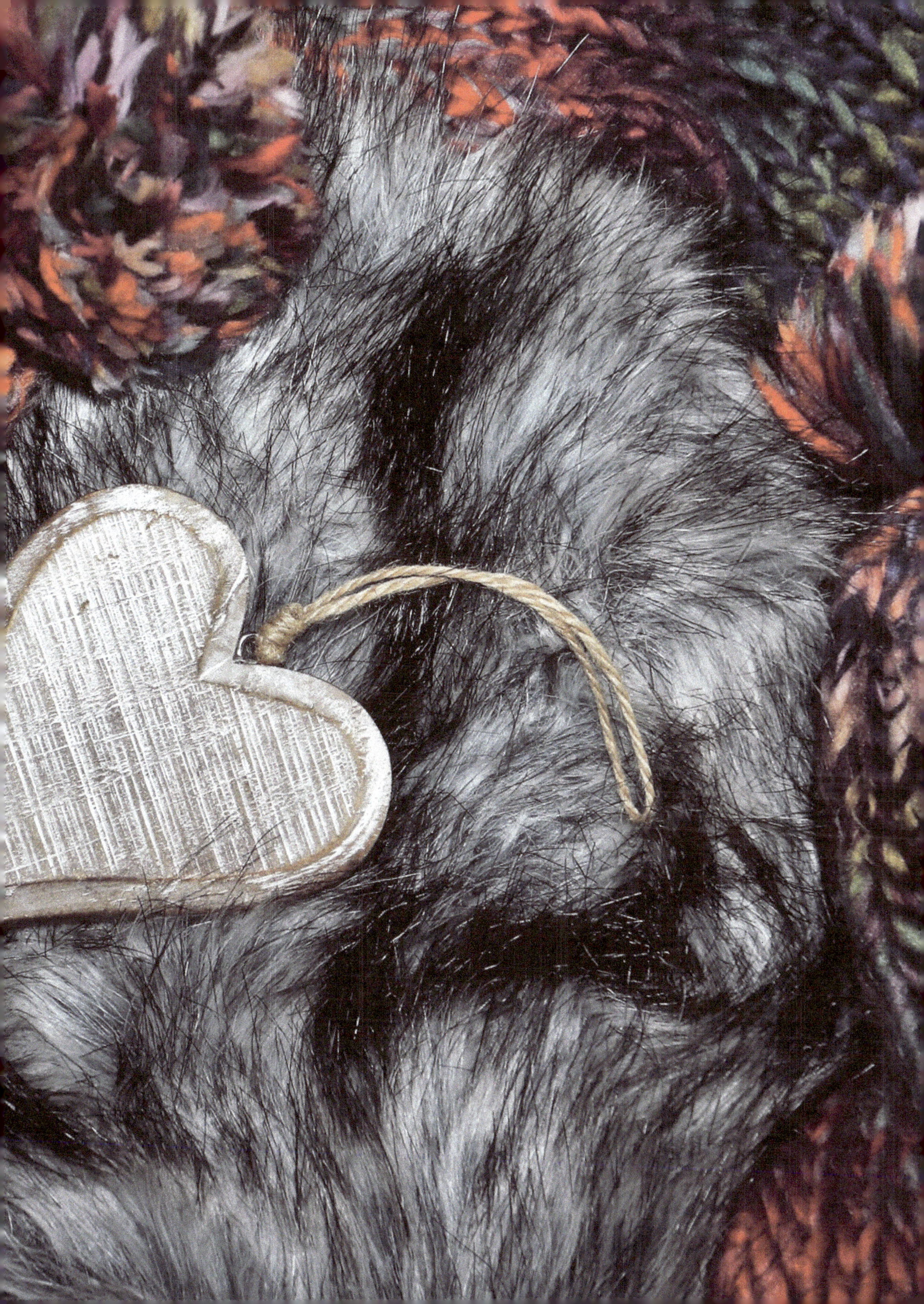

approach is more what you may be inclined to do, this approach will allow you to determine the demand for the designs you offer and plan the production accordingly. But selling online means challenging the existing competition!

Finally, suppose you prefer to sell your products online through an information network. In that case, you become an authority in the field, creating the opportunity to generate profit with your Cricut designs. By offering blogs on technical know-how or inspiration work, you become selective on the posts you want to take on.

Starting a new business requires foremost a business strategy, the foundation for your future success. Asking yourself who your potential customers would be, what kind of products you can sell them and how are the first steps of a future startup business. In terms of making money from the comfort of your home, you quickly achieve that with a Cricut machine.   However, you have to bear in mind that there are some competitors out there. Thus you have to put in extra efforts to stand a chance to succeed.

For you to become successful in the Cricut world of crafts, you have to keep the following in mind;

1. DARE TO BE DIFFERENT

You have to be yourself, unleash your quirkiness and creativity.

Those that have been in the Cricut crafts world for some time know all about the knockout name tiles. They became a hit, and in no time, everyone was producing and selling them.

In the crafting world, that is the norm. Thus, you

could be among the earliest people to jump on a trend to ride the wave until the next hot seller surfaces. Mind you, that strategy of selling Cricut crafts can become costly and tiresome if you are not careful.

The basic idea here is to add your flair and personal style and not to completely re-invent the wheel. For example, let's say you come across two name tiles on Etsy; one looks exactly like the other 200+ on sale on the site, while the second one has a few more tweaks and spins on it. The second product seller will possibly charge more and accrue a higher profit because his/her product is unique and stands out from the rest.

When you design your products, don't be afraid to tweak your fonts because even the simplest of tweaks and creativity can make your product stand out from the rest.

Remember this; if you create a product that looks exactly like others, you are only putting yourself in a 'price war,' where no one usually wins.

2. KEEP IT NARROW

Many crafters believe that creating and selling everything under the sun translates into more patronage and more money, but that isn't how it works. On the contrary, it might only result in a massive stock of unsold products, more burnout, and high cost. Rather than producing materials here and there, it would help if you focused on being the best in your area of craftiness so that when people need specific products in your area, they'll come to you.

It can be very tempting to want to spread your

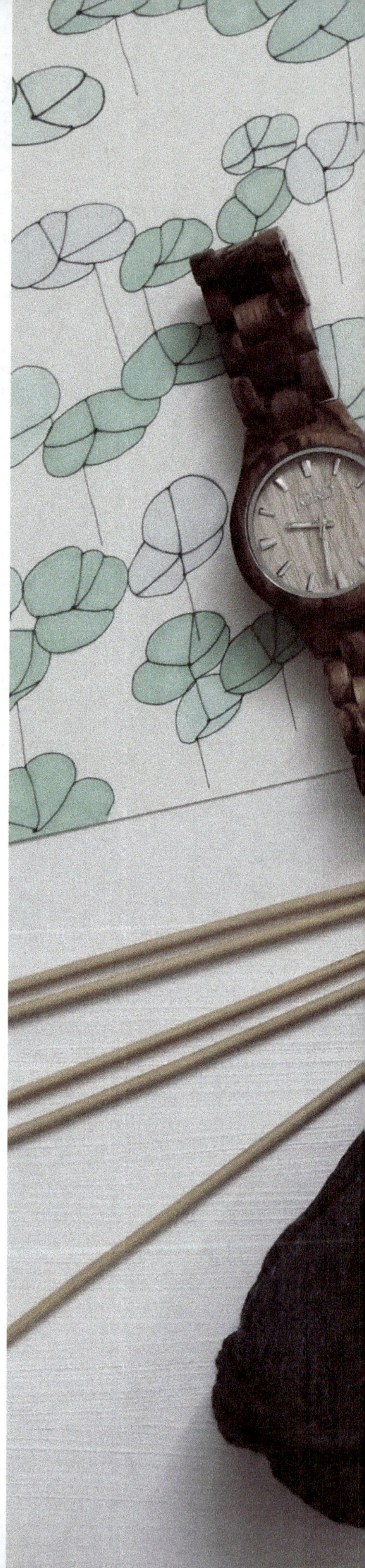

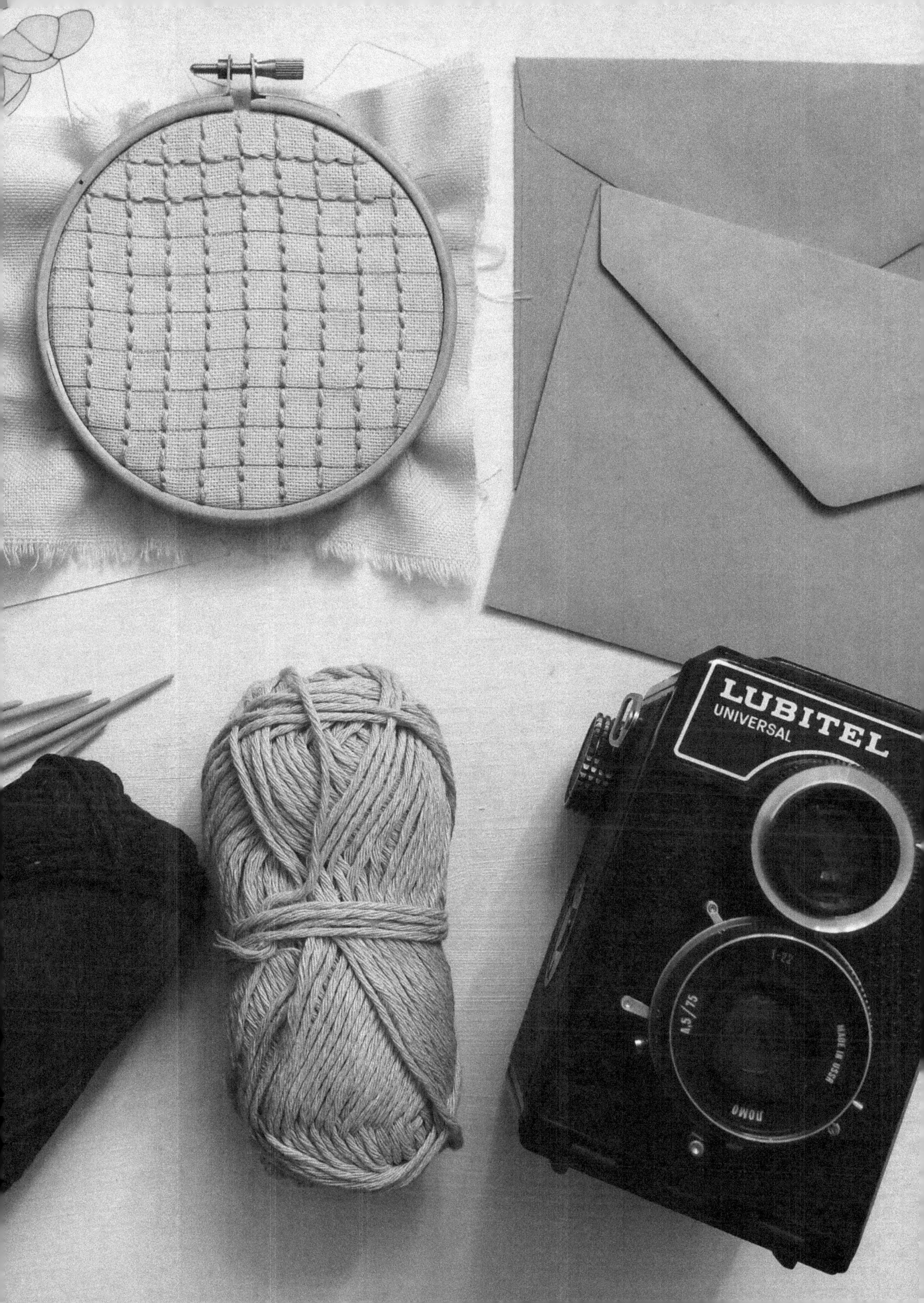
LUBITEL
UNIVERSAL

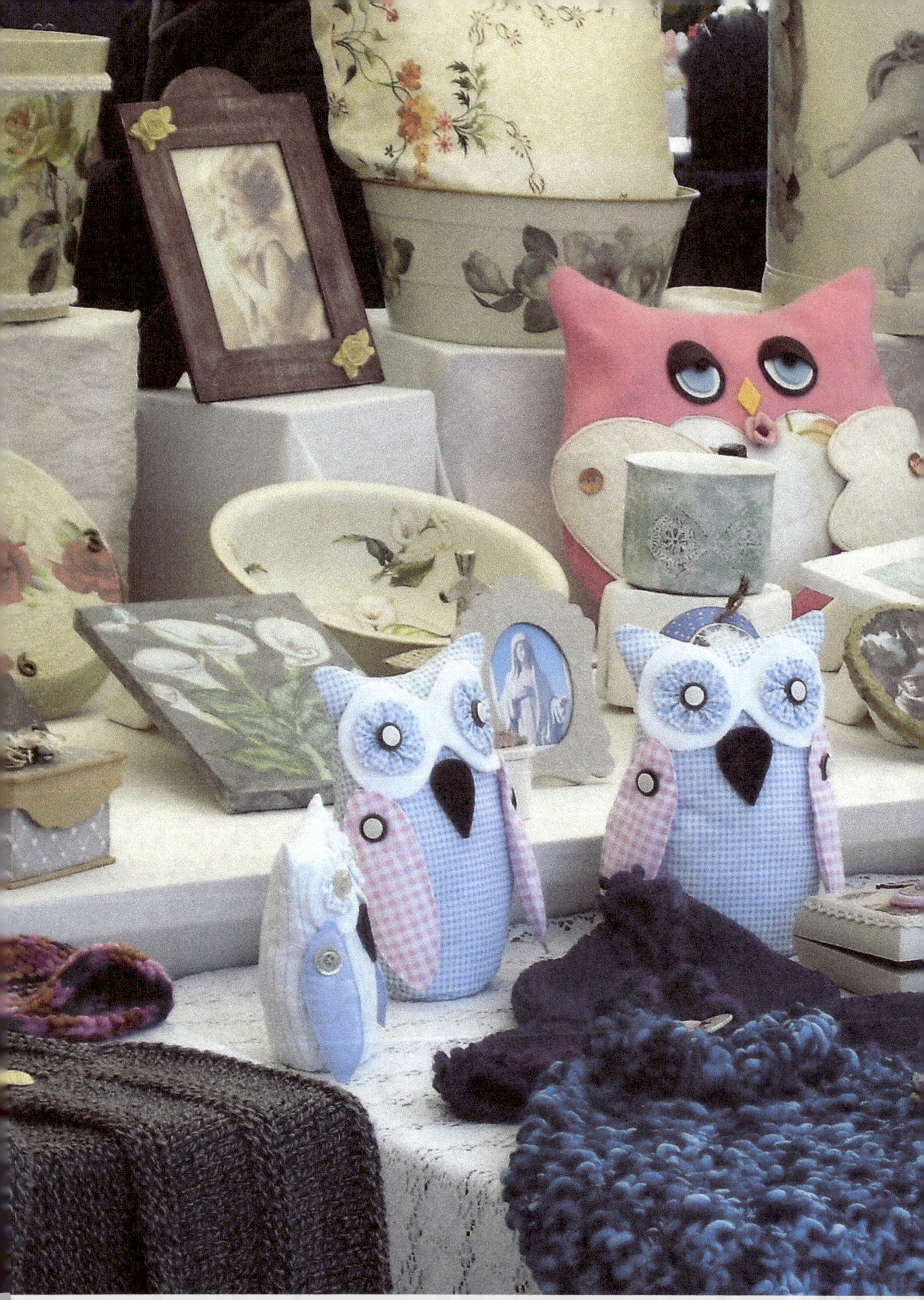

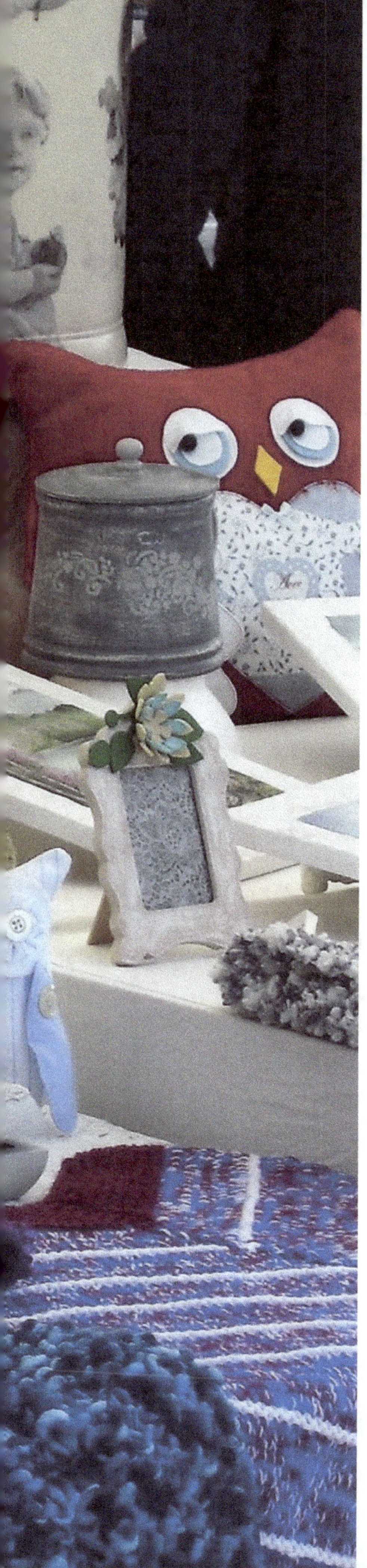

tentacles because it might seem like the more you produce, the more options you'll provide for your clients, but that might be counterproductive.

Take out time to think about your area of strength and focus your energy on making products that you'd be known for. It is better to be known as an expert in a particular outcome than to be renowned for someone that produces a high number of inferior products.

Thus, you should keep it narrow and grow to become the very best in your area of craft.

3. BE CONSISTENT

If you intend to become successful, you have to work on your Cricut craft business consistently. Some people work once a week or thereabout because they sell as a hobby; however, if you intend to make in-road in your business, you have to work every day.

If you have other engagements and can't work every day, you should create a weekly schedule and stick to it. If you shun your business for weeks and months at a time, then you will not go anywhere with it.

Apart from consistency in work and production, you also have to be consistent with your product quality and pricing. When your customers are convinced about your products, they will readily recommend you to their friends, family, business partners, and many others.

In business, there are ups and downs. Thus, you shouldn't reduce your work rate because things are not going as planned. Success doesn't come easy, but one of the surest ways of being and maintaining success is consistently doing the things you love.

4. BE TENACIOUS

It is not easy to run a business because it involves hard work, sweat, and even heartbreaks. Thus, you have to bear in mind that there will be days when you will feel like throwing in the towel. There will be days when nothing goes as planned. There will also be days when customers will tick you off. You will feel like a drowning boat because you're working hard, but nothing is working out.

However, you have to look at the bigger picture because the crafting business is not a get-rich-quick scheme. Remember, quitters never win, so quitting isn't an option. Keep doing the things you love and keep improving. Successful people never give up. They suffer many setbacks, but they don't stop. Thus, for you to be successful in your craft, you have to be tenacious and resilient. Be willing to maneuver your way through tough times, and do not forget to pick up lessons.

5. LEARN EVERYDAY

Be willing to learn from people that have been successful in the business. You don't necessarily have to unravel everything by yourself because whatever it is you are doing, others have already done it in the past.

Whether you intend to learn how to build a successful Facebook group or how to go up the Etsy ranks, remember that people have already done all that in the past and are giving out tricks and

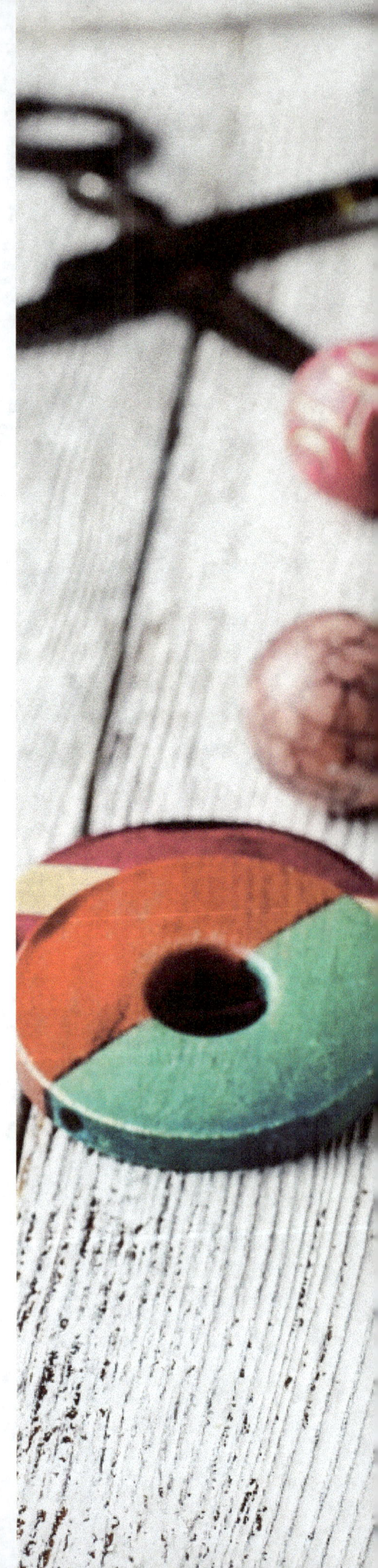

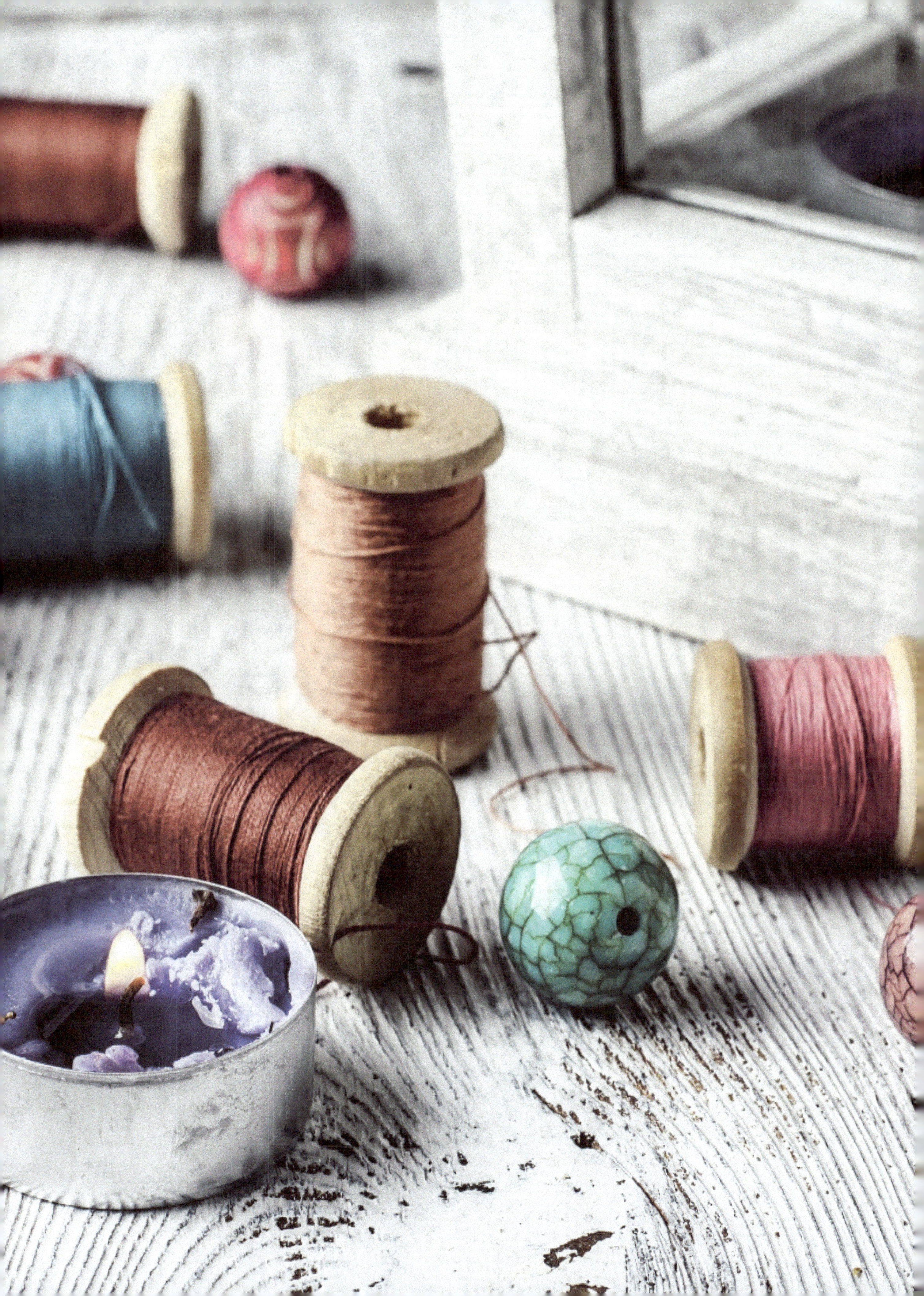

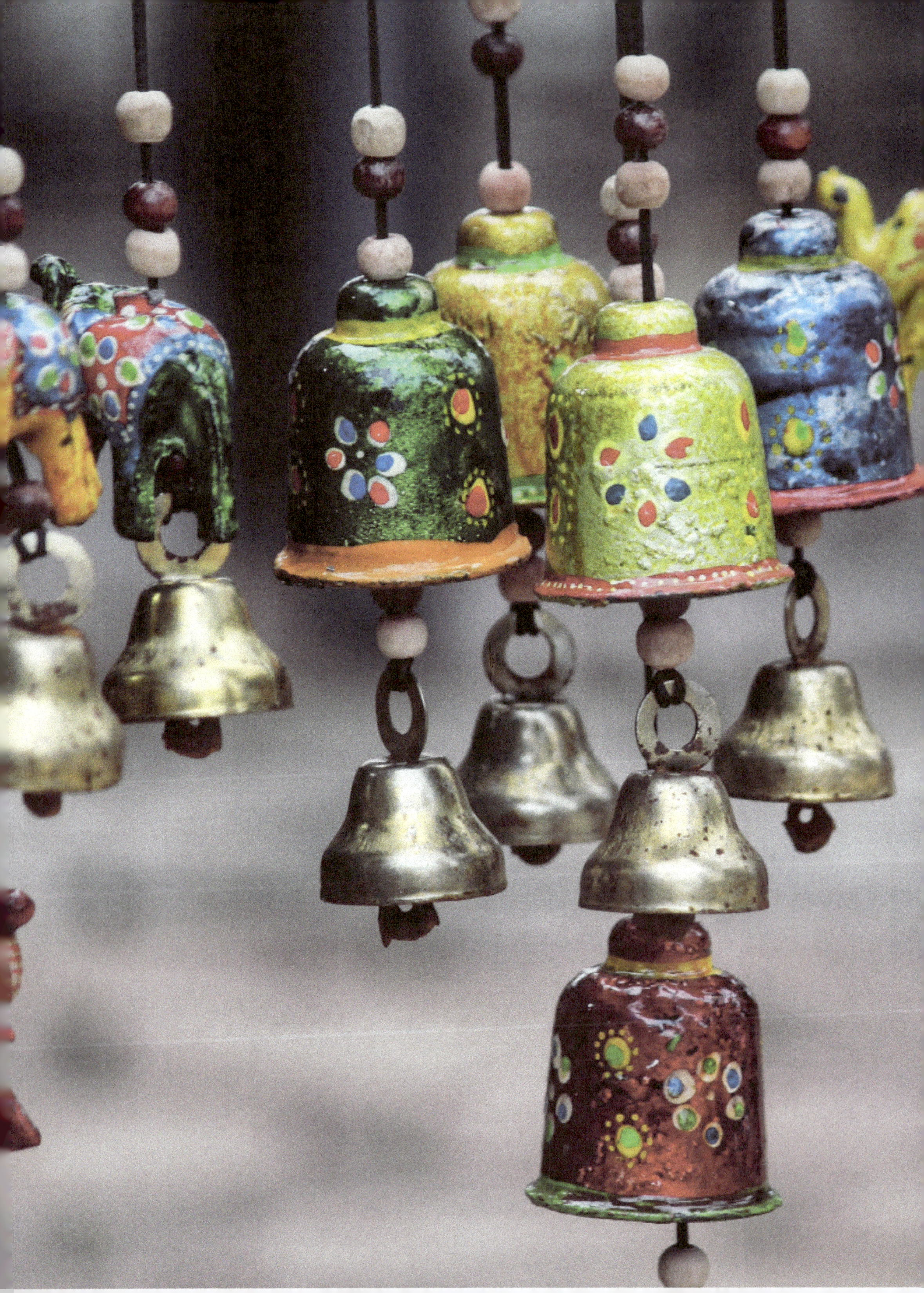

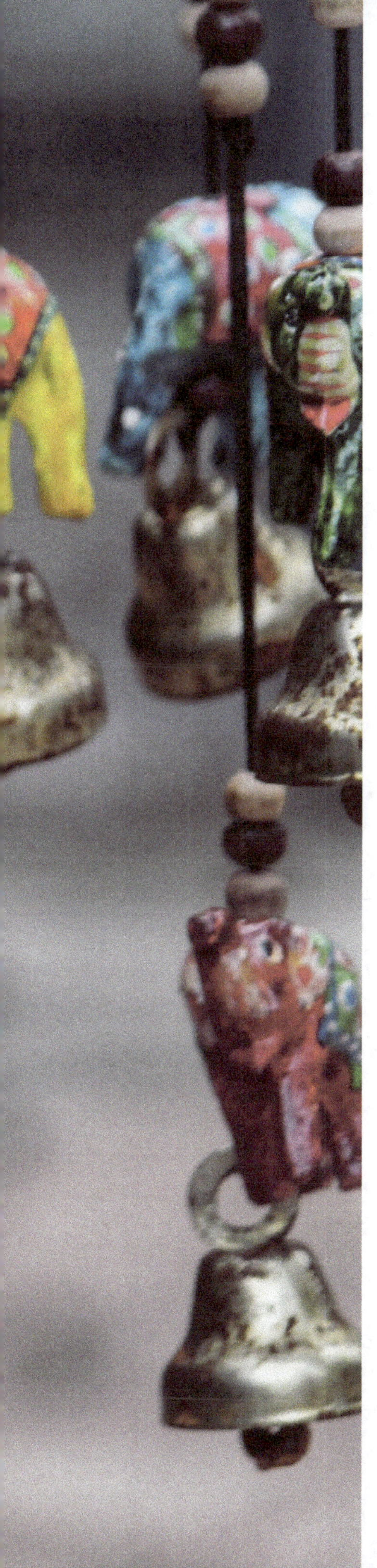

tips they know.

Make it a tradition to learn something new about your business every day because, at the beginning of your business, you will have to do more marketing than crafting.

When you wake up in the morning, browse through the internet, gather materials, and read in your spare time because the more you learn, the better your chances of success. They say knowledge is power. To become successful as a craftsman/woman, you have to continually seek new knowledge in tips, tricks, software upgrades, marketing, design ideas, tools, accessories, and many others. All I am saying is that you should learn without ceasing.

Conclusion

It's time to get crafting! Enjoy your new knowledge of your fantastic machine and give a new project a try. The beauty of the Cricut is the versatility of functions and user-friendly format. Use this to make your life and home and those of your friends and family more exciting and beautiful!

Using a Cricut maker machine should not be a new experience for you by now. However, it would be best if you kept an open mind to new updates. Cricut always gives its users many options to choose from, so try as much as possible to carry out extensive research about their products, materials, and subscriptions.

At this stage, we can both agree that Cricut offers a whole lot more than it requires. Do not give up trying to learn how to cut on Cricut machines. Although it might be a little frustrating getting design right sometimes, keep striving to attain perfection. You'll become professional in no time and probably start teaching other people how to use it.

Cricut machines are getting more popular every day. A lot of people have a preference for Cricut machines for many reasons. User-friendliness is one of the primary reasons that people choose Cricut machines to do their cutting job. It's easy to use and also easy to learn if you have the right resources. Almost anyone can set up a Cricut machine because it is not too complicated. All that a new user has to do is follow the straightforward instructions that come with the box.

There are so many amazing things that you can do with a Cricut maker machine. This book is only the beginning of what your creativity can do if you work with the Cricut machine. There are only new and better updates to the device, so now is the best time to get one and get in the door to understand what all it can do for you. We hope that the information we have provided you on what materials you can use with the machine, how to get your first project started, and all the project ideas are the tools you need to achieve the goals you have with the Cricut maker machine.

Keep this book handy as you start out working with your Cricut maker machine so that you always have a quick reference guide with you. This is an excellent way for you to get to know the device and not waste any time or material when you are just starting.

It would help if you were well equipped to make all of your dreams' projects, and you are well on your way to impressing your friends and family with your newly acquired skill of homemade gifts and décor. It would help if you also took the time to consider selling your projects to make a profit. You can have an excellent side business in no time that can help you pay for the machine and the materials you are using and put some extra money in your pocket to pay your bills or get additional holiday gifts. There are many bonuses to getting a Cricut maker machine, and we hope you have the opportunity to discover them all.

If at any point you get stumped on how to use your machine or are wondering what materials you should use, reference the previous chapters or visit cricut.com for help. Understanding and reviewing your Cricut maker's foundations is wise to make sure you are building on your skills with a solid foundation of knowledge. From there, your creativity can blossom, and the sky is the limit for what you can create. So now, stop reading and start doing! Make your first t-shirt design or hanging planter, and enjoy your creations.

I hope that you enjoyed this book and learned a lot!

Thank

you !!